The End of Architecture?

The End of Architecture?

Documents and Manifestos: Vienna Architecture Conference

Edited by Peter Noever
for the MAK-Austrian Museum of Applied Arts, Vienna

With a foreword by Frank O. Gehry
and contributions by Coop Himmelblau, Zaha Hadid,
Steven Holl, Thom Mayne, Eric Owen Moss,
Carme Pinós, and Lebbeus Woods

Prestel

This book is a documentation of the Vienna Architecture Conference, which took place on June 15, 1992, at the MAK-Austrian Museum of Applied Arts in Vienna. The architects' introductory statements and the subsequent videotaped roundtable discussion have been reproduced here as accurately as possible.

Concept: Peter Noever
Moderator: Frank Werner
General editor: Daniela Zyman
Photographic documentation: Michael Rathmayer
Video documentation: Monika Halkort
Editor of the roundtable discussion: Ziva Freiman

Cover: Lebbeus Woods, War and Architecture Series, 1992 (detail)

Photographic acknowledgments, see p. 135

Prestel-Verlag, Mandlstrasse 26, D-8000 Munich 40, Germany
Tel. (89) 38 17 09 0; Fax (89) 38 17 09 35

Distributed in continental Europe by Prestel-Verlag
Verlegerdienst München GmbH & Co. KG,
Gutenbergstrasse 1, D-8031 Gilching, Germany
Tel. (8105) 38 81 17; Fax (8105) 38 81 00

Distributed in the USA and Canada on behalf of Prestel by te Neues Publishing Company,
15 East 76th Street, New York, NY 10021, USA
Tel. (212) 288 0265; Fax (212) 570 2373

Distributed in Japan on behalf of Prestel by YOHAN Western
Publications Distribution Agency, 14–9 Okubo 3–chome, Shinjuku-ku,
J-Tokyo 169
Tel. (3) 32 08 01 81; Fax (3) 32 09 02 88

Distributed in the United Kingdom, Ireland, and all remaining countries on behalf of Prestel by
Thames & Hudson Limited, 30–34 Bloomsbury Street, London WC1B 3 QP, England
Tel. (71) 636 5488; Fax (71) 636 1695

Offset lithography by Repro-Center Färber & Co., Munich
Typeset and printed by Buch- und Offsetdruckerei Wagner GmbH, Nördlingen
Bound by Ludwig Auer GmbH, Donauwörth

Printed in Germany

ISBN 3-7913-1263-4 (English edition)
ISBN 3-7913-1268-5 (German edition)

Contents

Peter Noever — The Theme 9
Frank O. Gehry — Preface 11

Statements

Coop Himmelblau — The End of Architecture 17
Zaha Hadid — Another Beginning 25
Steven Holl — Locus Soulless 35
Thom Mayne — A Report from the USA 47
Eric Owen Moss — Out of Place Is the One Right Place 61
Carme Pinós — Following the Trace 73
Lebbeus Woods — Freespace and the Tyranny of Types 85

Roundtable Discussion 98

Biographies of the Architects 129

Peter Noever

The Theme

Spaces of desire in an epoch of extinguished utopias? **Programmatic programs** against the background of a society which has long since sought refuge in a general aesthetization of daily life, in a kind of irresistible folklore of consumption? The "Age of Conquest" it seems, has finally come to an end.

Strategies of resistance and postponement, the game with excessively complicated systems of decoration derived from an intertwining of diverse conceptions, the predilection toward material values – all this reflects how unreal our reality has become. A reality which blinds with its reproductions and castings, its devotional objects, and encoded, bombastic productions – which no one actually wants to have understood for what they really are.

A form of architecture is being developed worldwide, even by those who belong to the "Club of World Masters," which ignores actual, existing conditions, and allows no questions. Fundamental revisions of basic principles run aground on the disillusioned consciousness of our global culture. Most architects have lost sight of the mega-urban environment – the ghettos, crumbling walls, back alleys, makeshift residences under expressway overpasses, subway catacombs. Neither the nomadic nature of our industrial and leisure society, nor war, commerce, phallocracy, or general all-consuming chaos, have served as an impetus to discover new spatial organisms, new dimensions of space – to find a fitting architectural expression.

Today, anger and disappointment at the condition of our world have faded. In every conceivable field, marginalities seem to have become themselves the central themes. A collective production of technocrats, landmark preservationists, building and architectural firms, and politicians: high noon for unscrupulous adventures at breakneck speed!

Atrocities and audacious attacks on relevant architectural work are part of the daily news. Architects who attempt to practice real architecture have long been excluded from the discussion, as if forced into monastic refuges or exiled like medieval monks. Reactionary trends are springing up everywhere; there has been a tacit declaration of war against architecture. Thus the "Vienna Architecture Conference," to which I invited seven leading exponents of a new architectural spirit, was denounced in the press as a "secret meeting" before it even began. Of course, it wasn't a conspiracy; not even a secret gathering.

Moebius, *Histoire d'X*, (detail)

The Vienna conference, entitled "The End of Architecture?", was meant to serve as a forum for people of similar convictions to discuss this timely and explosive topic, with the intention of later compiling these discussions for publication. The book in hand makes it clear that a "cold" confrontation of diametrically opposing views would hardly have been conducive to understanding.

Ultimately, it seemed to me far more important to establish the differing positions and various approaches – differing with regard both to point of departure and method – of the architects who participated in the Vienna Architecture Conference, most of whom are labelled "Deconstructivists."

The result of these Vienna talks was – in some ways – a condemnation of anachronistic, sociopolitically indeterminate architecture – of slavish adherence to technology, formalism empty of content, galloping commercialism. The architects presented statements of various positions, affirmations of faith, provocations, and manifestos, ranging from the negation of the conventional term "architecture," to ways of adapting to the peripheral existence of those who are ignored, to poetic effulgences about the devastation of natural landscapes, to the practice of free, experimental architecture as a laboratory for creative thought.

Perhaps the Vienna Architecture Conference can be seen as an expression of the need to call a halt, as a return to the ascetic demand for Concept, for framing subjects in human terms, without shrinking back in fear at the subways or highways of the metropolis, nor allowing soulless "ghost cities," megalopolises, to come into being. Wherever there is war in the streets, be it in the Arabian desert or in the cities, villages, and mountains of the Balkans, individual solutions are no longer the answer: holistic thinking and collective issues have to move into the foreground.

The common denominator, the common objective, was architecture. Architecture today. Architecture as an expression of our age. Architecture – which can also be understood as a critical attitude, as the vision of a new way of thinking, sharply contrasting with the old.

Frank O. Gehry

Preface

The title "The End of Architecture?" fascinates me. It suggests that architects can decide when there is a beginning and when there is an end to architecture. Maybe the Pied Piper of architecture dances on to the scene and carries away with him all the architects in the world because society has been nasty to them. Yes, society has been nasty, but it has not singled out architects over others, as turmoil continues to dehumanize many parts of the world. I surely am not prepared to analyze the world at large, where it is going and what I should do as an architectural professional. It is easier for the people who choose not to build to reach for a higher moral plain. But architecture, after all, is about building buildings, and for buildings to be built, someone has to commission them and the people who commission the buildings have all kinds of agendas. When we are called upon to work for these clients, we must, on an individual basis, consider their agenda and determine if the project is appropriate to our individual values. It is at this critical point that we individually make our deal with the devil and then live with the consequences. The devil in each project comes with many faces – sometimes it is pure economic greed, sometimes it's self aggrandizement, sometimes it's political manipulation, or a variety of other faces. Architects usually sign on to projects full of optimism and hope. They look for loving support from their clients, enough money to make a living, and a heavy denial about how much devil exists in the equation. Most clients for architecture are decent human beings, well-intentioned, intelligent, who have to work within the constraints imposed upon them by the society around them. I have found in my own work that the healthy optimism when I start a project can be sustained to the end by involving the client in the thinking that goes into making the work. This results finally in the client becoming complicit in the decision-making process.

In listening to the tape of your conference, I kept wondering what you wanted to ask from the world. You all, in various ways, seem to suggest that something is missing and that perhaps an architectural position could be articulated which would clear the air. I remember feeling that way, but at this time in my life, it's simpler. I chose to be an architect because I wanted to build, and in order to build I have to build within the

social system. I have tried to put my cards on the table over the years and clarify who I am and what I am about so that certain clients who are interested in what I am doing have a target, and from that I get my work. Like all of you, I am left out of a lot of things. I guess finally I am optimistic that all of you will get work and will make beautiful buildings and will not have to sit around and worry about the end of architecture.

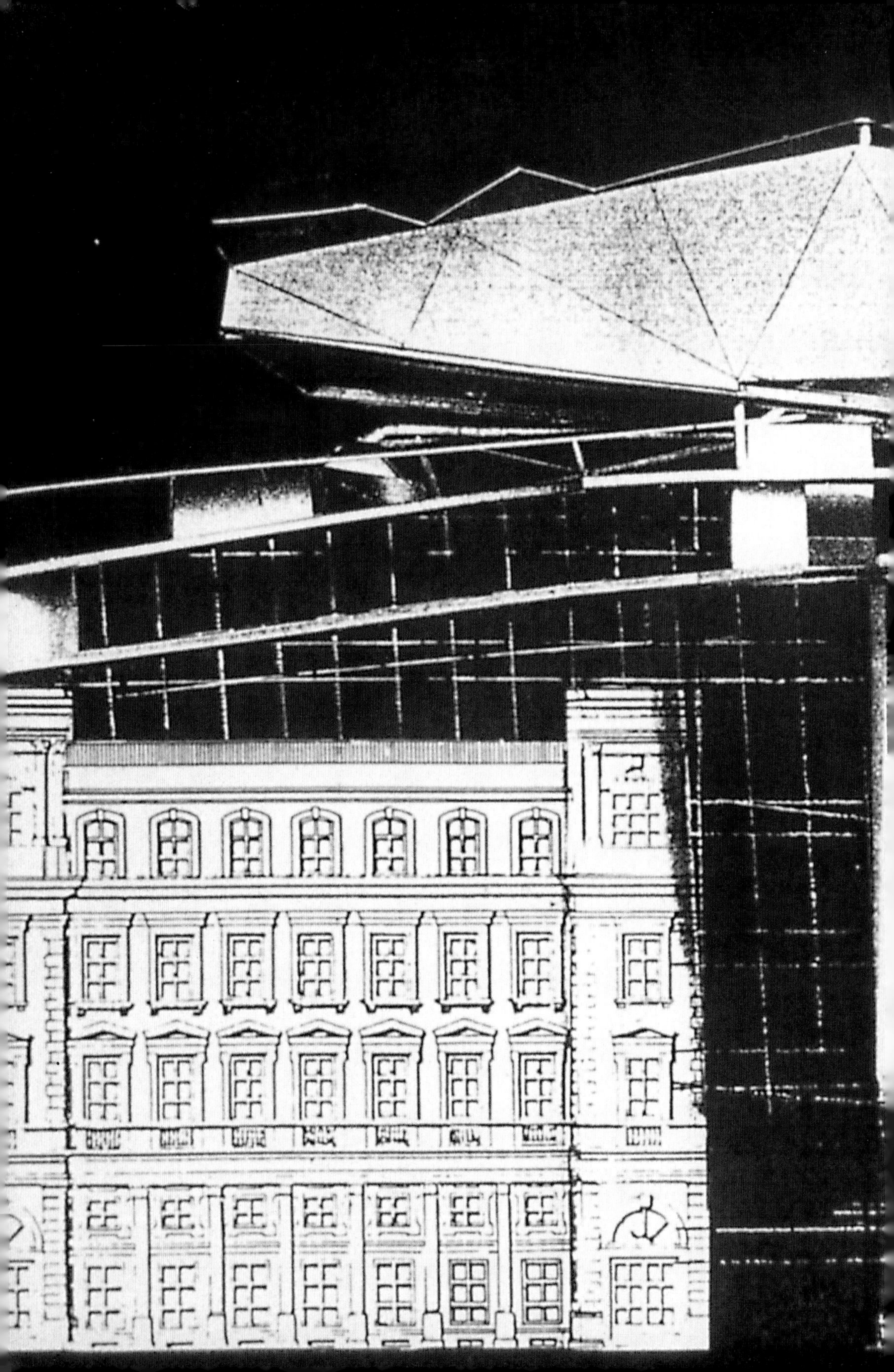

Coop Himmelblau

The End of Architecture

> Yes, the people that you mentioned I know them,
> they're quite lame. I have to rearrange their faces and
> give them all another name.
>
> Bob Dylan, "Desolation Row"

The Holocaust of Ideas

The mayor of Vienna gave two reasons why he was unable to continue to support a contemporary architecture project which had been five years in the planning (the Ronach Theater). These reasons were as follows: firstly, if he continued to support this project, he feared losing the support of his electorate, as the residents of Vienna don't want to see modern architecture; and secondly, there's in any case no more effective way to frighten the Viennese than to confront them with modern buildings.

One of the most controversial subjects of the present day, architecture is slowly beginning to supplant the visual arts in their wonted role as a provocative thorn in the side of society.

What's overlooked in this discussion is that, by rejecting contemporary architecture, society is losing its three-dimensional forms of expression. Not only does this represent a wanton destruction of creativity and energy; it means that, sooner or later, the third dimension will lapse into silence.

Uncomfortable, precise, self-confident energy will continue to be destroyed until it's replaced altogether by hastening, servile obedience.

Any critic of architecture who holds that an architect today is no longer an artist, but rather a manager; who understands architecture as a professional product which is easier to market the more neutral it is, is not only betraying the idea of modernity, but is contributing to an anonymous, speechless zeitgeist, reflected in the neutral spaces of its architectural constructions.

Neutral architecture as a neuter, as putty in the hands of developers, challenges one to rethink the meaning of the term "architecture" and, in the sense of a reciprocal confusion of terminology, to complete the building of this Tower of Babel.

This confusion of terminology leads to new definitions, and to destruction.

Architecture as a professional, lifeless product would be the holocaust of every spatial concept.

1
Revitalization of the Ronacher Theater, Seilerstätte, Vienna, 1989
First prize for revitalization, 1989
Total area: 34,386 sq. ft.

The Process of Design (An Interlude)

We believe our architecture to be the architecture of the next decade, perhaps even of the next millennium. It's an art which reflects the multiplicity and vitality, the tensions and complexity of our cities.

Our design methods describe an approach to the exploding core of a tension-laden field of complexity. And they culminate in a critical, explosive moment when everything that stands in the way of architectural freedom is pushed aside.

In this first stage, all of the contingencies inherent in the situation – clichés, guidelines and regulations, norms and functions – are excluded.

The rationalization and structuring of the concept, necessary for the actual building process, are the second step.

Since about 1978, we've gradually shortened and tightened up the time needed for this design process, without considering where this will lead us. That is to say, we discuss the project for quite some time, but without thinking of the tangible, spatial consequences.

Then, suddenly, a design is there. On a wall, on a table, on a piece of paper: somewhere. And always, at the same time, a model is built (though not to scale).

It works like this: Coop Himmelblau is a team. There are two of us. While we draw, architecture is expressed in words; the drawing is then narrated in the three-dimensional model. (Although we can't prove it, we strongly believe that the more forcefully the designer experiences the design, the more vital the completed space.)

In recent years, we've noted that, slowly but surely, we've begun to emphasize verbal descriptions of our designs by means of the gestures of our hands. Working on projects for Paris and Vienna, we found that it was body language which yielded the superior drawing, and the first model.

Desert Storm

This war, whose horrors were only perceived through the media, whose reality was therefore only a media reality, had the same relation to actual reality as a publicized, unbuilt project has to a completed building.

It isn't always important to build architecture. But sometimes it's vital. General interest in tangible, three-dimensional architectural creations is steadily decreasing. This is a result of the separation of head and body, thinking and being. Virtual space is becoming the sphere of activity for the life of the mind.

Such "mental" architecture resists its own realization. Its counterpoint, however, is not fragmented forms, negation, or displacement, but rather spaces which are simultaneously comprehensible and inapprehensible.

The Dissolution of Our Bodies into the City

As we began working on projects for the cities of New York and Berlin, the faces and figures of these cities became increasingly clear. We began by seeing and drawing the lines and surfaces of the city over a team photo of Coop Himmelblau. Our eyes became towers, our foreheads bridges, our faces landscapes, our shirts ground plans.

The lines and surfaces of the new structure, built as models, appeared more and more clearly; they became three-dimensional, casting shadows.

We love to design and make visible the unseen, actual, or possible lines and force fields of a city.

Just as we love to build buildings and their – constantly moving – shadows.

2–5
Dissolution of Our Bodies into the City, 1988

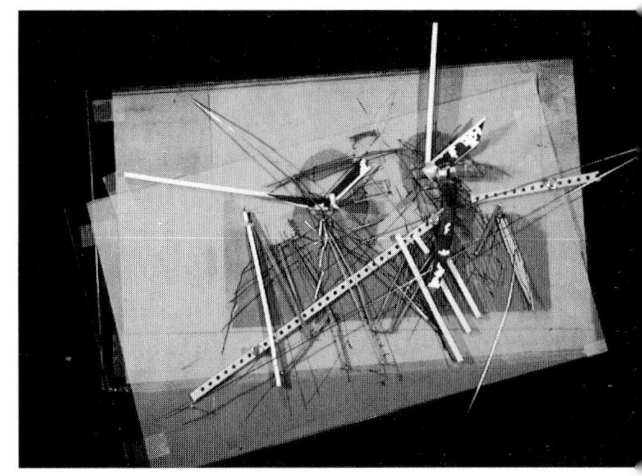

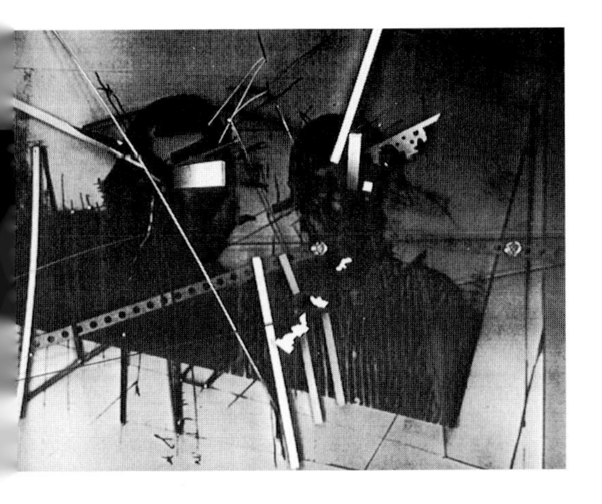

6, 7
Body Language, 1988

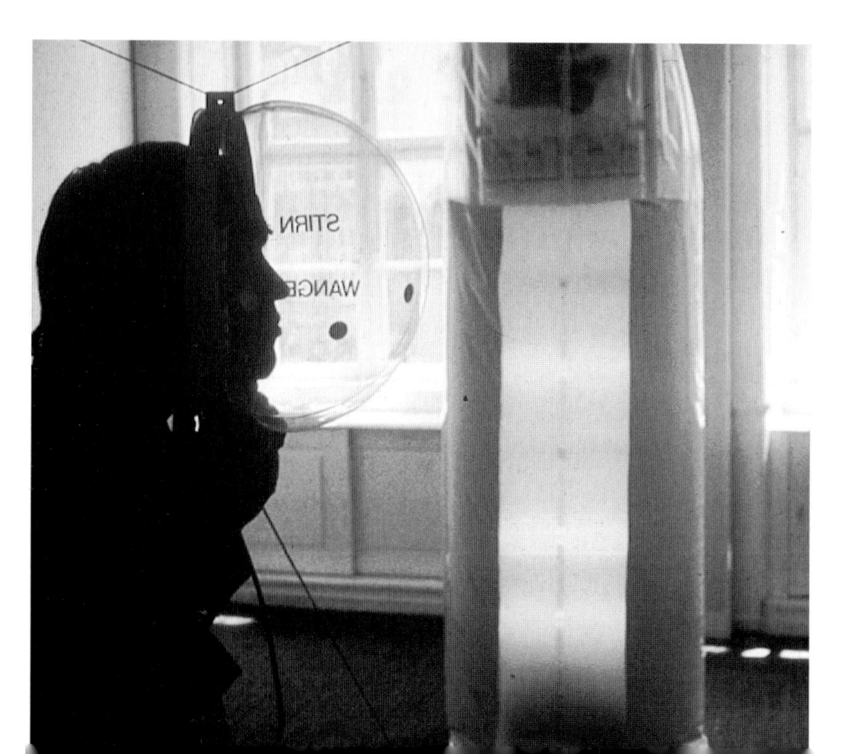

8
Soul Flipper, 1969
Mimicry, which is the external representation of a person's inner moods, is "objectified" in the "sound column." Laughter is translated into happy colors; the column radiates blue in the presence of a melancholy mood; and everything is underlined with an appropriate soundtrack.

9, 10
Hard Space, 1970
Three people set off sixty explosions each through their heartbeats alone. The explosives are planted in the landscape in three lines, each two kilometers long. One "space" is created within the space of twenty heartbeats.

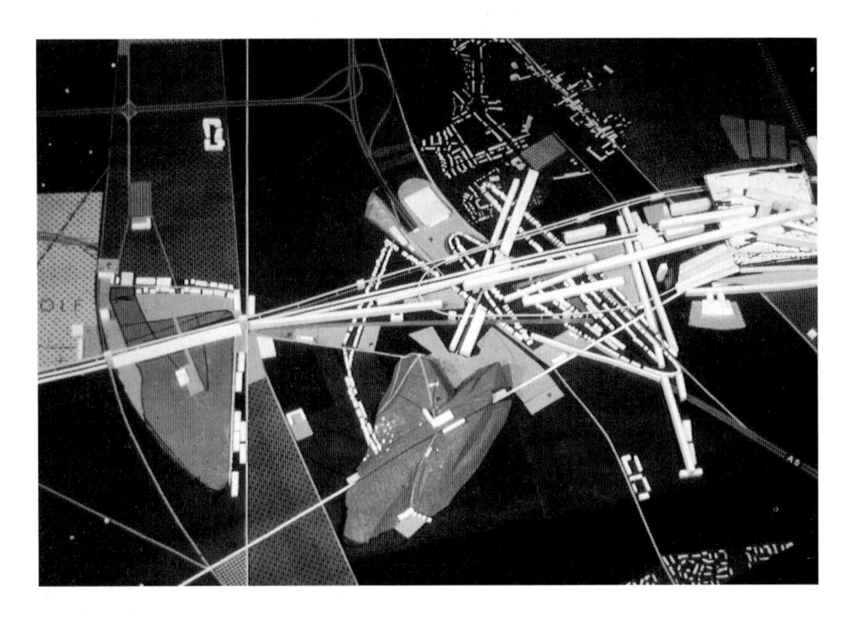

11
The Heart of Melun, Sénart, Paris, 1987
First prize at the International Town Planning Competition of Melun, Sénart, France
For us, a city is only a city if one can sense its multiplicity, its discrepancy. Highs and lows, fullness and emptiness, noise and quiet, heat and cold, tenderness and harshness, confusion and clarity, are all captured and preserved in structures which are at least theoretically possible.

12
Open House, Malibu, California, 1983
Total area: 330 sq. ft.

The feeling of the interior tautens the skin of the exterior. Created from a design drawn explosively, quickly, with closed eyes. Unbroken concentration, the hand as the seismograph of feeling, which calls the constructed room to life.

The house – tipped bodies, arched surface – measures 330 square feet. It can only be reached by means of a stairway.

The energy that flows through the drawing is translated into statics and construction. Supported at three points, the building almost floats. There are no prearranged divisions of living space. This can follow after the house is completed, or never: this, too, is open architecture.

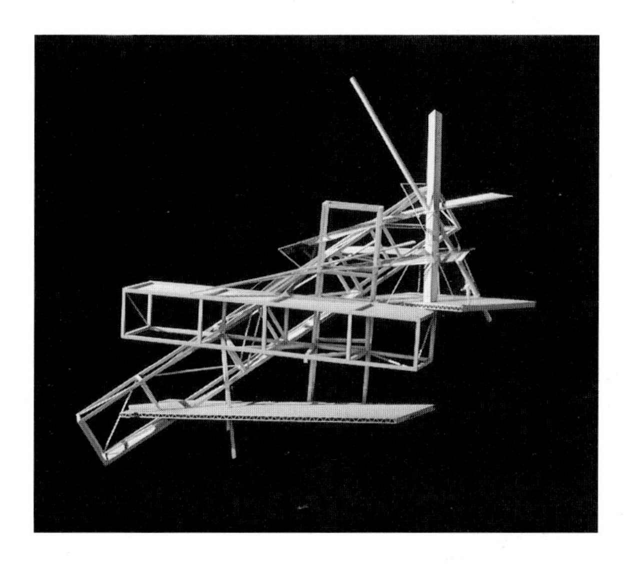

13–15
Rehak House, Malibu, California, 1990
Project architect: Frank Stepper

Zaha Hadid

Another Beginning

The conference posed the question "The End of Architecture?" as an investigation of the end of grand designs and big experiments. As the introduction points out, experiments exist now only as "exotic projects" in media niches. The media (magazines, exhibitions) are principally valid spaces for experiment, as long as they do not become an end in themselves. But when magazines and exhibitions become the sole context and *a priori* aim of architectural experiments, these experiments cease to be architectural ones – or rather, they cease to be experiments of any kind as there is no longer any real objective. An experiment for the sake of experiment is a contradiction in terms. Nevertheless, this is the vanishing point of the current architectural discourse at the opposite pole of current architectural activity. As "experimentalism" mushrooms, real experiment vanishes.

As actual professional practice becomes ever more circumscribed by codes, standards and stereotypes, architectural education – the arena of the experimentalist fringe – becomes ever more unrestrained in its self-indulgent "radicalism": this is the inverse-proportional flipside of the same development. As London exemplifies, the most restrictive practice is the breeding ground of the most irrelevant experimentalism in education. A rift has opened up, which leaves the student unprepared and impotent to challenge the profession into which he or she is thrown. The result is business as usual.

1
Vitra Fire Station, Weil am Rhein, Germany, 1990–92
Project team: Zaha Hadid with Patrik Schumacher, Kar Wha Ho, Voon Yee-Wong, Nicola Cousins, David Gomersall, Signy Svalastoga, Simon Koumjian, Cristina Verissimo, Maria Rossi, Daniel Oakley, Edgar Gonzales, Craig Kiner, Diane Hunter-Gorman

The concept of "the end of architecture," the demise of grand design and experiment, implicitly contrasts current architectural culture with the heroic period of Modernism. Thus to explain the current "end..." we need to analyze the context and condition of the Modern Movement and so identify the crucial economic and political changes since that time.

It has often been pointed out that the Modern Movement had a social commitment. But this social commitment was not due to the honorable idealism of the architects which has since been rarefied. Rather, it was a reflection of the political transformations after the First World War. In Germany, for instance, a revolution had taken place, and a social-democratic government was promoting public programs involving architecture as part of the construction of a new society. In the young Soviet

Union, the relationship between architecture and society was even more outspoken. The new, real possibility of grand projects created the context of the even grander, but always relevant, visions of architects like Le Corbusier, Hilbersheimer, and Leonidov.

At conferences like CIAM (Congrès Internationaux d'Architecture Moderne, founded in 1928), far-reaching visions were related to the tasks posed. The discourse was an organic part of a collective practice. Here, in the realm of public projects and urbanism, the path-breaking heroic propositions for a new architecture were inspired and fulfilled. The masses became architecture's new client. Especially in the Soviet Union, new programs (like the workers' clubs) inspired new architectural forms. In New York, the dense layering of new programs found a distinct architectural expression.

Similarly, after the Second World War, the flourishing discourse and practice of urbanism in general (around groups like Team X, which arose from CIAM X held in 1956), and the creation of specifically new forms of housing were inspired and grounded by huge public building programs. The welfare state was inviting architects to rethink and reconstruct the human environment on a comprehensive scale.

The ideas of social progress and of man's ability to consciously construct his or her social world seem discredited today. Grand designs (as well as "grand narratives") are seen as nothing but grand pretensions, hubris with fatal consequences: "the fatal conceit."

2
Vitra Fire Station, Weil am Rhein, Germany, 1990–92

The post-war welfare state – with its ambition to democratize and consciously plan more and more aspects of social and economic life – has collapsed, and is seen as a fatal hubris of tampering with the "natural" course of things. The concept of comprehensive planning is discredited in economics as well as in urbanism; restoration and tradition have taken its place.

The very notion of design – in the sense of a fresh, methodical application of human reason to a given problem – has become problematic and is seen as no match for the process of natural self-regulation (economics), natural growth (urbanism), or natural adaption and development as represented by traditional forms of building. What the Enlightenment regarded as prejudice came to pass as the unmatchable cumulative wisdom of time itself.

Did the twentieth century really expose the inherent limits of human reason? The opposite is the case: democratization and, through it, the conscious and rational organization of society did not go deep enough, so that the people's palaces turned into ghettos and modern architecture became unwittingly their unlucky symbol. From the late seventies onwards, the public sector was deteriorating, discredited, and then actively dismantled. And with it went the public projects and the public role of the architectural profession.

The new role of the architect is to comply with competitively asserted standards of efficiency, to cater to commercial clients, increasingly with the objective of representing corporate identity or else of satisfying the fluctuating standards of good taste. The profession is thus torn into two distinct aspects: on the one hand, architecture becomes a pure technique, as if it were a branch of engineering; on the other hand, it becomes image-production, as if it were a branch of advertising. It is the rise of this second role which is the half-conscious background to the recent flourishing of "experimentalism" in architecture.

The conference's theme alludes to the fact that architecture for architecture's sake no longer predominates, and it now seems that only fashion is being rewarded. Architecture for architecture's sake cannot be the solution, cannot be the antidote to fashion; only a social purpose to architecture, publicly formulated, can be such an antidote. There can be no great architecture without a social program. A visionary architecture has to take part in a political vision, and its reality presupposes a political process which puts a new architecture on the agenda and thus transforms the profession into a movement with new aims and inspirations. (The ironic contradiction here is that democratization of design itself would, artistically, lead to mediocrity.)

Such conditions are lacking today. The current economic role of the architect produces, at one pole, docile, alienated technicians and, at the opposite pole, a star system promoting individual artists like brand names with a marketable value. The "discourse" deteriorates into a disparate juxtaposition of commodified monologues, where the market value of each "philosophy" depends on the effective devaluation of the competing brands.

Where does this leave committed architects who are not willing to accept the end of architecture after all? If they are compelling enough to reach the status of "artists" within this system, they might still be able to expand the architectural vocabulary and explore new ways of translating complex programs into meaningful, three-dimensional compositions – i.e., artists should still be able to pursue their more general and forward-looking agendas within the frame of private commissions. A serious drawback is that new forms without new programs and new ways of (social) life have a hard time transcending formalism. And the struggle is hard and lonely, and one is permanently in danger of running out of resources. This requires nearly superhuman self-discipline since, despite all the publicity surrounding the artist, one is not really exposed to the productive critique of authentic and focused public debate.

Experiments will really bear fruit on a wider scale only if such explorations are focused by publicly posed tasks and conducted within an architectural community that operates in productive cooperation, rather than the antagonistic competition fueled by zealous insistence on privately marketable identities. The masses have to become once more the client of architecture. But these cannot be the culturally excluded masses of today's increasingly divided society; in this society, the architect still needs to hope for an enlightened patron.

3
View from The Peak into the public void, Hong Kong, 1982
Project team: Zaha Hadid with M. Wolfson, J. Dunn, M. van der Waals, N. Ayoubi

4
The Peak above the city
of Hong Kong, 1982

5
View from The Peak
into the public void,
Hong Kong, 1982

6
Trafalgar Square Grand Buildings Project, London, 1985
Early stages with Brian Ma-Siy
Competition team: Michael Wolfson, Brian Ma-Siy, M. Palme, Kar Wha Ho, P. Smerin
Perspective view in city context; detail

7
Trafalgar Square Grand Buildings Project, London, 1985
Perspective view in city context

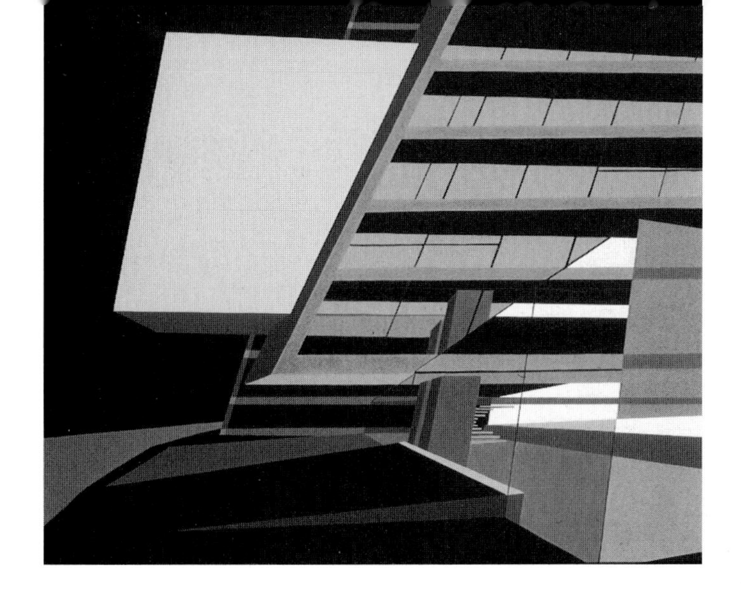

8
Kunst- und Medienzentrum Rheinhafen, Düsseldorf, Germany, 1989–92
Project team: Zaha Hadid with Brett Steele and Brian Ma Siy, Yousif Albustani, Tuta Barbosa, Paul Brislin, Cathleen Chua, John Comparelli, Elden Croy, David Gomersall, Craig Kiner, Graeme Little, Paco Meijas, Daniel Oakley, Sophia Psarra, Patrik Schumacher, Alastair Standing, Signy Svalastoga, Ademir Volic
Construction team: Zaha Hadid with Michael Wolfson, Edgar Honzales, Craig Kiner, Patrik Schumacher, Ursula Honsior, Bryan Langlands, Ed Haskin, Yuko Moriyama
Entrance

9
Kunst- und Medienzentrum Rheinhafen, Düsseldorf, Germany, 1989–92
View into interior space

10
Kunst- und Medienzentrum Rheinhafen, Düsseldorf, Germany, 1989–92
Overall plan

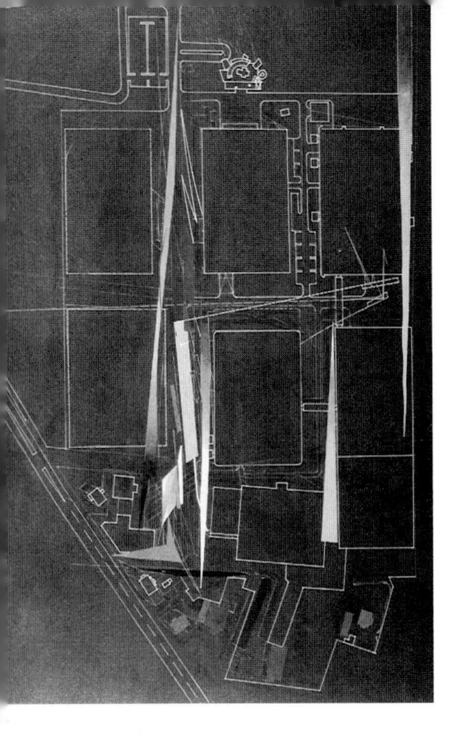

11–14
Vitra Fire Station, Weil am Rhein, Germany, 1990–92
Site plans and detailed sketches

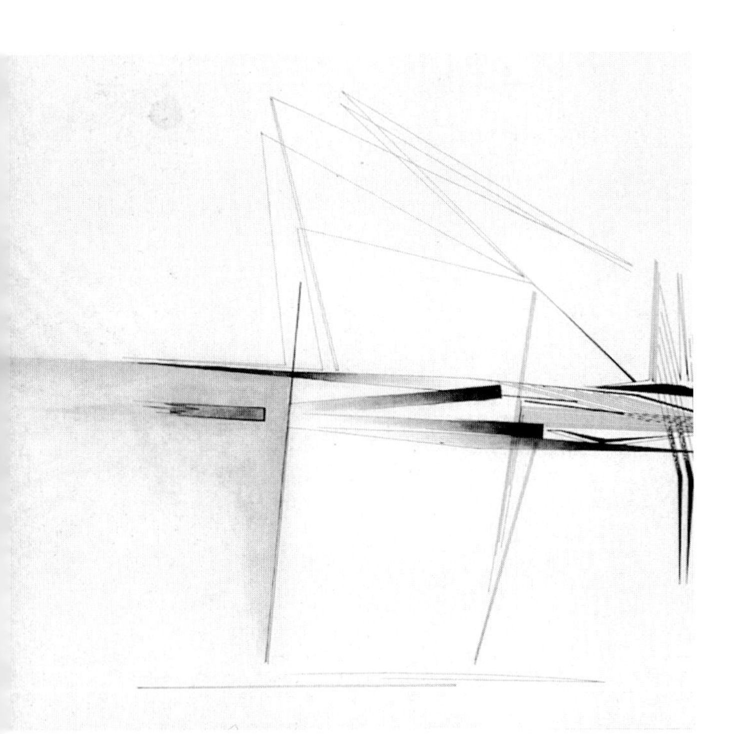

15, 16
Vitra Fire Station, Weil am Rhein, Germany, 1990–92
Exterior views

Steven Holl

Locus Soulless

1
D. E. Shaw & Co. Offices, New York, 1991
Project architect: Thomas Jenkinson
Project team: Scott Enge, Todd Fouser, Hideaki Ariizumi, Adam Yarinsky, Annette Goderbauer
Spatial color reflection

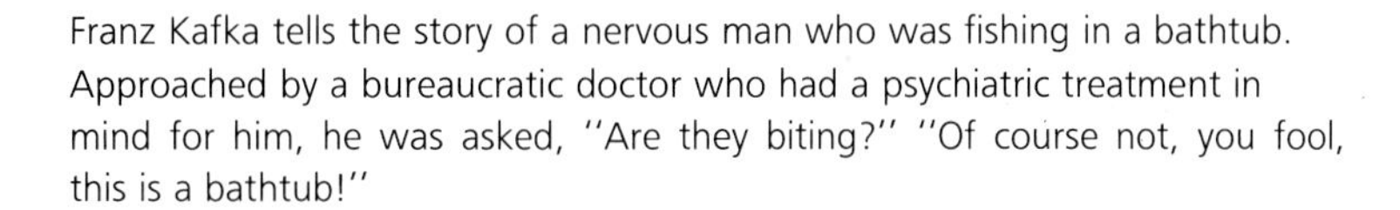

Franz Kafka tells the story of a nervous man who was fishing in a bathtub. Approached by a bureaucratic doctor who had a psychiatric treatment in mind for him, he was asked, "Are they biting?" "Of course not, you fool, this is a bathtub!"

From relatively flat terrain, or from a boat on the ocean, the visible horizon is about three miles in the distance. In a color photograph on a magazine page, or on a video screen, the horizon is collapsed in a two-dimensional frame of simulation. Yet this graphic horizon line, among a field of electronic impulses, is part of a continuous flow of information, a global network of exchange.

This repetitive, omnipresent field of rays has expanded exponentially in a very few years, displacing the machines of industrialization. Paradigm shifts comparable to those of the beginning of the twentieth century seem imminent.

2
African mud sculpture

While a global movement electronically connects all places and cultures in a continuous time-place fusion, the opposite tendency coexists in the uprising of local cultures and expressions of place. In these two forces – one a kind of expansion, the other a kind of contraction – new types of space are being formed.

In the locus of this field of expansion with its counterpoints of contraction, we can either attempt a new architecture or remain victims of the nervous impulse of media and homogenization to minimize and slacken the spirit. Undirected expansion of technology leads to a soullessness, oblivious to location and individual. Simply to mirror fragmenting and conflicting forces is a style of architecture for a trend in time rather than a particular program and place.

First I would like to make some observations, pose a few questions, and then offer three examples of projects in which I hope to fuse different spaces of expansion and contraction, flow and location.

As in Ovid's *Metamorphoses*, "Knowledge of the world means dissolving the solidity of the world." So in the paradigm shifts of today all material heaviness seems to disappear. The devices propelling this world of information-flow utilize non-material impulses in a visual field. Computer-aided design, motion control, virtual reality, magnetic resonance imaging, computer animation, synthetic holography – to name a few of the present means – are all rapidly developing vectors of information which are characterized by motion and light.

Positivist traditions of western rationalist materialism uncritically drive societies into a space of optimization and flow of capital, while the obliteration of place continues to drain the world of individual significance.

The horror of current events are projected into domestic living-rooms everywhere. Likewise, a soulless fashionable commercialism characterizes many of the arts. As we allow ourselves to be victims of unconscious habits, skipping from gesture to final image, we leap over the simmering of feelings and thoughts that carries a slow-developing intensity of ideas and forms and their interior spatial consequences.

More than anything, the conception and development of architecture takes time. Architecture likewise has the capacity to measure time, and to adjust to the programmatic flux of a society in dynamic change.

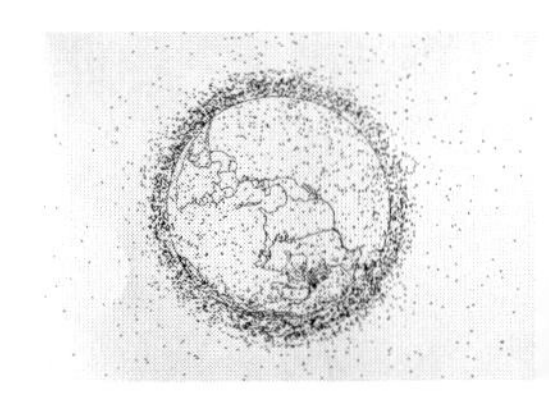

3
Field of flow-space debris

4
Robot sumo wrestling

In recent decades, the devices of technology have continuously shrunk, becoming silent and invisible. This miniaturization and tendency to disappear is technologically a new path, displacing the machines in Siegfried Gideon's thesis of 1947, *Mechanization Takes Command.* The slow, anonymous, industrialized reshaping of daily life by various physical machines was documented by Gideon in drawings and photographs. Instruments of mechanization gradually took on a dominant physical presence. Optimization and repetition in technique produced machine "types" instead of individual works. The architectural style "High Tech" is unrelated to the actuality of technological miniaturization and invisibility, as well as being generally oblivious to place. "The split between thought and feeling," an issue which Gideon felt was the urgent focus, remains. It has widened.

Rather than a surrender of technological transformation to expressions of place or vice versa, a non-dialectic relation might be sought. Working with doubt allows an acceptance of the impermanence of technological change, while opening up to metaphysical particularities of place. A way of holding these two opposed realms together with precision is characteristic of an architecture of clear ideas rather than of compromise.

The space of expansive flow has an ambiguous continuity, while spaces of differences have distinct irregularities. The politically controlled space of commodity-exchange in a world market is part of the homogenizing efforts of states. This is an abstracted space, continuous and in layers. On the other hand, the spaces of natural origin, cultural origin, or ethnic group have particular physical climates, ecological uniqueness, and topographical differences.

An architecture fusing these worlds of flow and difference is inconsistent by nature. As the differences of individual circumstance are essential, this architecture must accept Emerson's admonition, "consistency is the hobgoblin of little minds." Rather than conforming to technological or stylistic uniformity, this architecture would be open to the irrationalities of place. It would resist the homogenizing tendencies of standardization.

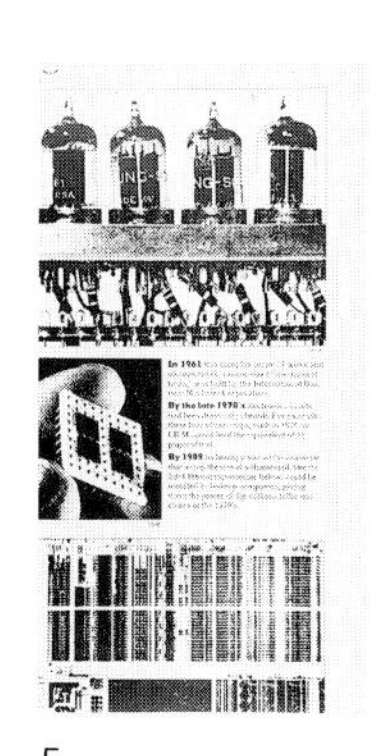

5
Miniaturization

Hybridization would be a general consequence in seeking a new unity of dissociated elements in architecture. Hybrid building programs, with their mix of living, working, culture, and recreation, break down the social barriers of rationalist zoning. Experimental hybrid construction techniques as well as detail explorations would take this hybridization to the micro level of an architectural construction and the experience of detail and material.

The barrier between public and private, like the barrier between flow and location, would be another realm for transformation. With advanced technological means, the abstract space of a world market would be available to ethnic groups who, gaining individual strength, could restore their cultural and natural resources.

By thinking of these forces as simultaneous expansion and contraction rather than as progression and regression, a non-dialectic relationship is established. The contraction phase is allowed to telescope into the expansion phase, and vice versa. A new architecture must be formed that is simultaneously aligned with transcultural continuity and with the poetic expression of individual situations and communities. Expanding towards an ultra-modern world of flow, while condensing into a box of shadows on a particular site, this architecture aspires to William Blake's admonition "to see the universe in a grain of sand." The poetic illumination of unique qualities, individual cultures, and individual spirits makes reciprocal connections in the transcultural, transhistorical present. In the project examples that follow, various degrees of relation to site and to technological flow are explored.

Parallels to invisible technology were investigated in an interior for D. E. Shaw & Co. on the top two floors of a skyscraper in Manhattan. This experimental project explored the phenomenon of spatial color reflection, or projected color.

D. E. Shaw & Co., a financial trading firm formed by a doctor of physics, works with the minuscule drift of numbers and percentages measured in short intervals of time. The firm's computers are connected to financial markets by satellite and by telephone lines, executing trades globally 22 1/2 hours per day, at rest only between the close of the London markets and the opening of the Tokyo exchange. One room in the facility contains more than two hundred computers.

This curious and invisible program has a parallel in the design concept of the interior. At a thirty-one-foot cube of space at the entry, the walls are carved and notched to create gaps and fissures through which other spaces may be viewed. Color has been applied to the back or bottom surfaces of these notches, and is projected into the space by daylight and

6–8
D. E. Shaw & Co.
Offices, New York,
1991
Spatial color reflection

electric light. Only the projected color is seen; the actual colored surface remains invisible to the viewer. As reflection greatly reduces the intensity of color, a range of intense fluorescent colors could be utilized on the unseen surfaces. While the perimeter of the offices has dramatic views of Manhattan, this inner cube of space is introspective. The interior has a mysterious calm glow, with surprising views as one moves around observing one field of reflected color through another. The invisible, untouchable, projected color is the manifestation of the electronic flow of the exchange.

In the project for a house with a particular connection to its Dallas, Texas site, the concept of flow was explored, based on the overlapping musical form known as "stretto." Sited adjacent to three spring-fed ponds with existing concrete dams, the house projects the character of the location in a series of concrete block "spatial dams" with metal-framed "aqueous space" flowing through them. Like the stretto in music, the water flowing over the dams is an overlapping reflection of the space of the landscape outside, as well as the virtual overlapping of the space inside.

In particular, Bartok's *Music for Strings, Percussion and Celeste* was the parallel on which the house form was made. In four movements, this piece has a distinct division between heavy (percussion) and light (strings). Where music has a materiality in instrumentation and sound, this architecture attempts an analogue in light and space, i.e.:

$$\frac{\text{material x sound}}{\text{time}} = \frac{\text{material x light}}{\text{space}}$$

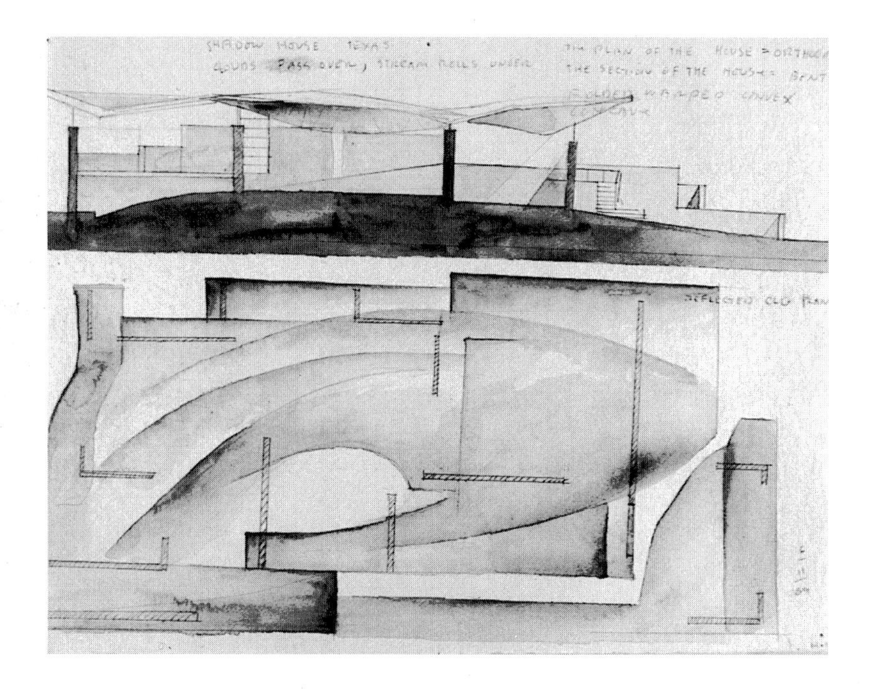

9–12
Texas Stretto House, Dallas, Texas, 1992
Project architect: Adam Yarinsky
Project team: Peter Lynch, Bryan Bell, Matthew Karlen, William Wilson, Stephen Cassell, Kent Hikida, Florian Schmidt, Thomas Jenkinson, Lucinda Knox
Cross section; model; detailed view; fountain

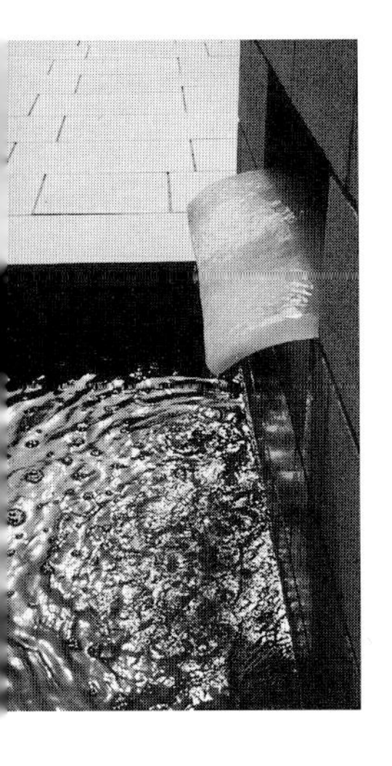

The building is formed in four parts, each consisting of two modes: heavy orthogonal masonry, and light and curvilinear metal (the concrete block and metal of Texas vernacular). The plan of the main house is purely orthogonal and the section curvilinear; the guest house is an inversion, with the plan curvilinear and the section orthogonal, similar to the inversions of the subject in the first movement of the Bartok score. In the main house, aqueous space is developed by several means: floor planes pull the level of one space through to the next, roof planes pull space over walls, and an arched wall pulls light down from a skylight. Materials and details continue the spatial concepts in poured concrete, cast glass in fluid shapes, slumped glass and terrazzo.

Arriving at the space via a driveway bridging a stream, the visitor passes through overlapping spaces of the house, glimpsing the flanking gardens and arriving at an empty room flooded by the existing pond. The room, doubling its space in reflection, opening both to the site and to the house, becomes the asymmetrical center of two sequences of aqueous space.

The last illustration of a project simultaneously about technological flow and particular place is a competition entry for the Palazzo del Cinema in Venice. The new building site beside a lagoon on the Lido is to have six separate cinemas, the largest with 1,650 seats. The connection of the Lido site to Venice by water is emphasized by a grand arrival of space on the lagoon, a place for the Lido community filled with diaphanous light from gaps between the cinemas above. During the months when there is no cinema festival, this public grotto might have shops along the arcade or marina functions coexisting with the Palazzo del Cinema.

Time in its various abstractions link architecture and film. The project involves three interpretations of time and light in space. *Collapsed and extended time* within film is expressed in the warped and extended weave of the building, analogous to film's ability to compress (twenty years into one minute) or extend (four seconds into twenty minutes). *Diaphanous*

13
Palazzo del Cinema,
Venice, Italy, 1990
Competition project

14
Palazzo del Cinema,
Venice, Italy, 1990
Light reflections in the
grotto

time is reflected in the sunlight dropping through fissure space between the cinemas into the lagoon basin below. Ripples of water and reflected sunlight animate the grand public grotto. *Absolute time* is measured in a projected beam of sunlight which moves across the "cubic pantheon" in the lobby.

The projection of light in space, light in reflection, and light in shade and shadow is seen as a program to be achieved parallel to solving functional problems.

A vessel for "filmic time" and "filmic space," the building perimeter is bottle-shaped, with the mouth open to the lagoon towards Venice. The cinemas interlock within this frame, creating essential crevices and fissures which allow sunlight to the water below. In section, like interlocking hands, the cinemas turn slightly, changing their interior and exterior aspects of space.

The lobby at the end of the covered boat basin joins arrival from the east with arrival from the west. Escalators take people with tickets to the upper level lobby which has a café and a horizon view of the Adriatic. The escalators pass through the lobby space in sections like the weave of the theaters over the lagoon. The main facade of cable-reinforced sand-blasted acrylic responds to this warp and weave.

The main structure is of concrete in "planar" form. Metal formwork for the concrete is retained on the exterior face. Made of a brass alloy, this metal acquires a red patina over time.

In some areas the cinema screens can be withdrawn, and the cinema images projected onto warped concrete planes of the structure itself,

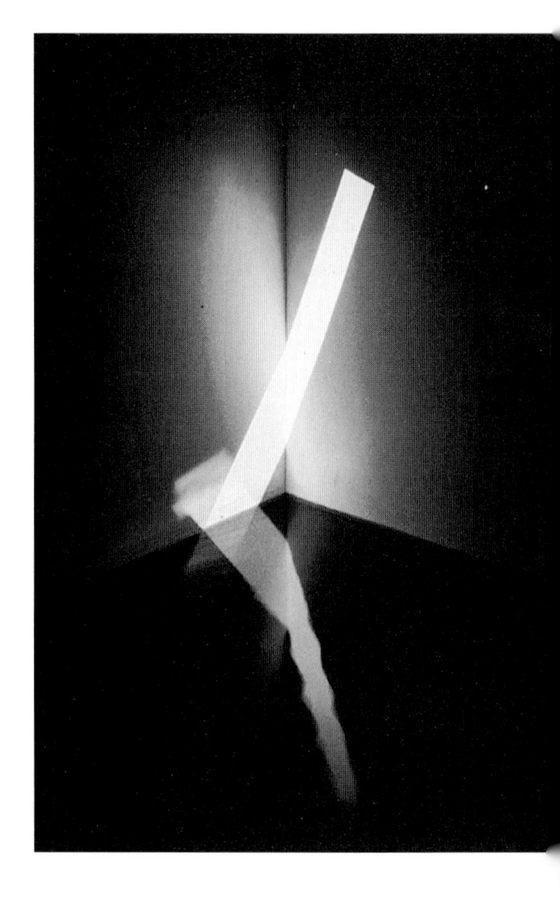

showing them as dissected colors and light on the exterior. The monolithic red patina of the exterior is interrupted by these warped projection zones – here, cinema burns holes in architecture.

Day and night are celebrated. During the day, light is projected from the outside in, between cinemas, onto the lagoon water, and through the light slot into the cubic pantheon. During the night, light is projected from inside out, through the baffles behind the cinema screens, through the translucent facade, and onto the boat basin from the lobby.

15–17
Palazzo del Cinema, Venice, Italy, 1990
Models

A retractable fabric roof allows for the large cinema to be open to the night sky. In the future, the advent of "cine-holography" would allow for hemispherical projections in the sky when the roof is retracted.

The new Palazzo del Cinema attempts a phenomenological link between film and architecture: a heightening of awareness of human experience in time, light, material, and space is offered as a parallel to "filmic" time.

> a slow cascade of light drops
> between the lips of the crannies
> Light is water; water, diaphanous time
> Where eyes wash their images
>
> Octavio Paz, *A Draft of Shadows*

NORTH ELEVATION 立面図

Thom Mayne

A Report from the USA

No one would have thought of fighting for the rights of a pure, denatured, universal subject – a subject whose value is not determined by race, creed, color, sex, or station in life – no one would have thought of waging a war on behalf of liberty and justice for all subjects, if Descartes had not already isolated for us this pure, abstract instance in whose name the war would be waged: the democratic subject, devoid of characteristics. This is surely the source of America's self-proclaimed "radical innocence," this belief in a basic humanity in which this nation's diverse citizens share.[1]

1
Joan Copjec, *The Urban Text.*

A colleague of mine recently related an experience of having been passed over by a jury for the commission to design a public building in Los Angeles. He was told by one of the jurors what had occurred in the process of their deliberations, that the decision to eliminate his team came about by a consensus among them that "his articulation of a position (and its implication of an architecture) was problematic." Probing further, he came to understand that the jury saw itself as representative of a tremendously diverse constituency and was expecting the *process* of realizing the building to be extremely difficult. Whether the members of the jury felt factionalized among each other was not clear, but that they expected difficulties from opposing interest groups was unmistakable. Their primary responsibility was, as they saw it, to resolve this situation by selecting a neutral solution – a work which would not offend. They felt that to choose an architect with a *point of view* was to guarantee failure, so the commission was awarded to the firm that represented the least possible threat within a consensus framework. They were hopeful that the input from the various factions during the design process would be enough to guide the work to a *satisfactory* outcome. Any discussion of the broader questions inherent in the context of this project would be suppressed by the operational strategies required for its realization.

The issues brought up by this jury are symptomatic of the broader political conditions that confront us today, particularly in the USA, where there is a general lack of will to confront our contemporary urban prob-

1
Nara Convention Center, Nara, Japan, 1992
Project architect: Mark McVay

lems. Although the relationship of architecture to its immediate political and economic context is elusive and complicated, we have no choice but to ask fundamental questions which redefine our intentions and our methods of intervention.

What are the issues which these questions address? First, it is important to articulate and define the public versus the private nature of our work and to develop some effective conception of space as a necessary social condition. Second, it is necessary to develop methods of articulating idiosyncracy. Modernism's proposal, situated within the twentieth century's social/economic framework, advocated standardization and serial production. Under the auspices of an aspiration for greater unification, similarity was privileged over difference, thus suppressing diversity. The importance today is to comprehend and utilize the complexity of everyday experience. Third, there is our need to interpret our time *authentically*. Architecture's recent intoxication with literal historical precedent has shown us the hopelessness of such regressive strategies in the face of the magnitude and complexity of our cities (in both a political and an architectural framework). It is necessary for architecture to be based in the present and to aspire to that presence.

The Public Realm

> On August 23, 1966 at 6:35 GMT, the ground control center in California radioed instructions to the photo satellite, Lunar Orbitor I, revolving around the moon, to glance back at its home planet. For the first time in history, man saw, even though only through technical servo eyes, his own earth as a celestial body.[2]

2
NASA.

Our understanding of the world today has radically realigned our perceptions of our human interactions. The methods by which we formulate our interests and values are now defined within a global context. The current definition of community has limited validity, as our associations with our neighbors are no longer based on common interests within the physical geographic domains of the conventional neighborhood, but are based increasingly on global connections.[3] People have any number of *interactions* which are not dependent on face-to-face physical proximity. One of the consequences of this breakdown of a conventional notion of community is the loss of a cohesive concept of a public role, accompanied by the continued advancement of the private persona. One of the possibilities that grows out of this condition is an architecture which oscillates between these two poles, maximizing their conflictive status.

3
Truett Anderson, in *Reality Isn't What It Used to Be*, discusses globalization as providing a new arena in which all belief systems look around and become aware of all other belief systems, and in which people everywhere struggle to define who and what they are.

About Diversity

> True freedom is not freedom from constraint, but rather to be constrained only by what one really is, by one's essence.[4]

Philosopher John Dewey maintained that engaging the rough grain of differences in things is the great moment of truth in art. Instead of focusing our discussions on universal intentions and meanings, the architect must pay attention to the specific materials which will give intentions concrete life. As with art, the experience of diversity in a city will make a more developed human being. Our society is subject to enormously varied and complex stimuli in its economic, political, and erotic life. Yet both the codes of inwardness and unity that have shaped our culture make it difficult to cope with the importance of diversity. We have trouble understanding the experience of difference as a positive human value.[5]

The potential of the modern dynamic ought to take a particular and human form, turning people outward. The movement away from a way of life as essentially simple and orderly to a view of life as complex and ironic is what every individual passes through in becoming mature.[6] The essence of development as a human being is in developing the capacity for ever more complex experience. Conventional ideas about city planning tend to be about a simple order (homogeneity). Present urban experience contradicts this – it desires to be defined through oppositions and disjunctures. Gleick's "Chaos Theory" suggests that ordered systems arise spontaneously out of conditions that look chaotic, but which really harbor hidden ordering principles. The true revelation of chaos studies is not that order appears out of real chaos, but that some systems that appear chaotic are actually just complex systems.[7]

Our new conceptual attitudes must embrace difference (the product of the complex systems that constitute our urban environment). Our modernist penchant for unification and simplification must be broken. And this, then, is the key issue – the recognition that *diversity* is the natural order of things. To accept this dynamic state rather than looking to replace it with something fixed, stable, whole, is to utilize the tremendous energy of the city.

The Need for Authenticity

What is ironic in a time of unprecedented advancement in scientific and technological inventions is the reactionary and superficial appropriation of historical forms. The problem here is not just one of form, but of the tendency for this architecture to be acquiescent to the day-to-day demands of utility and economics. This linkage of a benign architecture passively serving a status quo society is what is so apparent in our current situation.[8]

4
Erich Fromm, *Escape From Freedom*.

5
Richard Sennet, in *The Conscience of the Eve*, goes on to discuss the immersion into this unknown quality of the city in order to sense the other, "to understand *we*, we must do the work of accepting ourselves as incomplete ... it is out of the harsher connection made out of the arousal by the stranger, the feeling of the presence of those who are different that lets us know ourselves. Experiences of immediacy become intertwined with those scenes on the street which tend to fragment one's vision ....

6
Richard Sennet, *The Fall of Public Man*.

7
Gleick, *Chaos, Making a New Science*.

8
One of the architectural consequences of this situation is that so much recent work is about surface and image, preocuppied with the physiognomic. The content has become ephemeral, readily consumable, a product of the neglect of the material qualities of the work. The retention of literal physicality will be one of the great crises of architecture in the coming century.

The culture of our cities is now overtaken by a frenetic reach for the *past*. One wishes to live in one's grandmother's house at the point at which it is impossible to empower oneself even to envision, much less create, a house of one's own. The past is romanticized, seen as a place of safety and security to one who feels intrinsically unsafe. That we are frightened of our world and see it as threatening is made abundantly clear by reviewing the plethora of architectural projects which have been realized to create an ersatz cultural experience.[9] What is revealed in these schemes is a deep poverty of the imagination which is founded on a superficial understanding of what it is that gives life to a city. Clearly, our turn to the past and to this false experience seems to epitomize the cynical attempt of a rational age to cover up its own poverty. We do not feel confident that we have a vision of our own which can (and must) be created, so we look back, hoping compensation will be found in the riches of the past. This romanticizing of the simple life fails to grasp that it is in the realization of complexity and contradiction that we begin to find our way out of the psychological malaise we are currently suffering. It is nurturing an eye for the idiosyncratic, the phrases left unspoken, the unfinished, that allows us to utilize the potentiality of our cities.

9
Hal Foster, in *Recodings: Art, Spectacle, and Cultural Politics*, reminds us that these historical images, like mass cultural ones, are hardly innocent of their associations. It is precisely because they are "so laden" that they are used. Such architecture stratifies as it juxtaposes, reaffirming some past social order along with its underlying privileges.

10
Siegfried Gideon, *Space, Time, and Architecture*.

A Critical Optimism

Twenty years ago, a British scientist named James Lovelock described an imaginative and lyrical theory of how the earth functions. His idea was that the organisms on the planet work together to regulate the global environment. The earth itself, he said, appears to behave like a living organism. It may have its own self-preservationist strategies that are not apparent to us (yet). Is it possible, then, to imagine that this organism goes through periods of illness and recovery, building up immunities, adapting as it grows? Could the organism suffer from temporarily debilitating conditions such as depression, or anxiety, or psychosis? I find this metaphor seductive because it allows me to imagine that the malaise we currently suffer may be temporary; the organism may recover if we treat it correctly. So, for the sake of argument, I imagine the organism to be suffering from a state of psychological depression. The jury in Los Angeles, whose comments were related earlier, is just one source of this observation. Their comments were rife with evidence of a depressive mind-set. The diagnosis of depression is complex, but some of the major clues are extreme lack of self-esteem, anxiety, fearfulness or panic in the face of new experience. Feelings of worthlessness and fear often lead to a self-destructive despair.

Gideon has talked of our time as suffering from its inability to control or organize (artistically) the possibilities that it has itself produced.[10] Modern urbanism has provided the world with a vast legacy of diminished expectations; if architecture has a single objective, it is to clarify its intentions and realign its purposes with the aim of combating formlessness.

The modern, dystopian city will overlay differences rather than segment them. We will hold to that which is difficult, because it is difficult – and by its difficulty is worthwhile. A city is a living organism, a work-in-progress, an impasto of forms made by successive waves of habitation. One should continue to choose to do only those projects which offer hope of a complex, integrated, contradictory and meaningful future.

Will people like or even understand the work implied by this agenda? When did any new architecture fail to raise hostility? When does anything new find instant acceptance? There is always a psychological resistance to change – to a new way of seeing, feeling, and perceiving that breaks with the past. The work that follows explores and maximizes the conditions of heterogeneity emanating from conceptual strategies affecting the organization of objects and space. The following four projects attempt to frame these issues from two perspectives. The first relates to culture, specifically in an attempt to define an appropriate context. The second is concerned with the integration of architecture and nature.

What Man Has Done from the Beginning

The Gatehouse for Cranbrook College returns to a primitive architecture of the land. Man's impulse throughout the ages, in both the eastern and western civilizations, to mark the earth as a way of communicating is fundamental. Earth scratchings, rearrangements, scrapings, and other markings on a scale larger than that which can be understood in situ are documented from the earliest civilizations. Such strategies challenge us to reconsider the assumptions we make about time and space as we move in our everyday worlds. The Gatehouse project may be understood through its architectural language; it is light, topography, ambient noise, the spaces *between* things, and the nature of their relationships that are the raw materials we use to create this dialogue. The Gatehouse fragments, as objects, cannot be understood fully outside their positions within the manipulated elliptical earth surface. Through this arrangement we see the site anew; unexpected beauty and ever-changing patterns affected by time appear in the everyday places we thought we understood.

The choice of site for the new Gatehouse complex is one that by its nature is displaced from the campus. This factor underlies the basic premise of our design strategy, in which we have chosen to accentuate the condition of physical dislocation, while simultaneously emphasizing the connection to the campus through both direct physical relationships and more indirect psychological associations. We have created a *place* by augmenting and reshaping the natural landscape. The Gatehouse is one of a series of objects which occupy this space, and can be understood as a fragment of a thick zone or vertical layer of the elliptical space. The Gatehouse is oriented within the ellipse parallel to the highway, while the elliptical space as a figure is oriented on the same cardinal grid as that of the campus.

Lacking a close physical proximity to the campus, we aspired to create a place which would engender a sense of recognition for those approaching the campus. The boundary or edge condition of this site, in relationship to the campus, is established by the penetration of the access/egress road into the space and its vertical displacement along this edge. The alternating series of objects and spaces evoke a sense of progressive thresholds and enclosures producing a sequential experience of passage. One's experience upon entering the campus through the Gatehouse is that one is entering over a threshold marked in the ground by an incision which is covered with a metal grate. There is both an auditory and a visual demarcation as one drives across the threshold. The lantern gives a reflecting opacity or a semi-transparency by day, while at night it is perceived as a translucent glow.

The experience of entrance and exit are differentiated. Those entering are directed along the edge of the space and under the glass lantern overhead. The site is tipped towards those entering by a 1.5 degree slope, foreshortening the space and allowing one to perceive the nature of the sequencing of foreground and background. Those exiting the campus

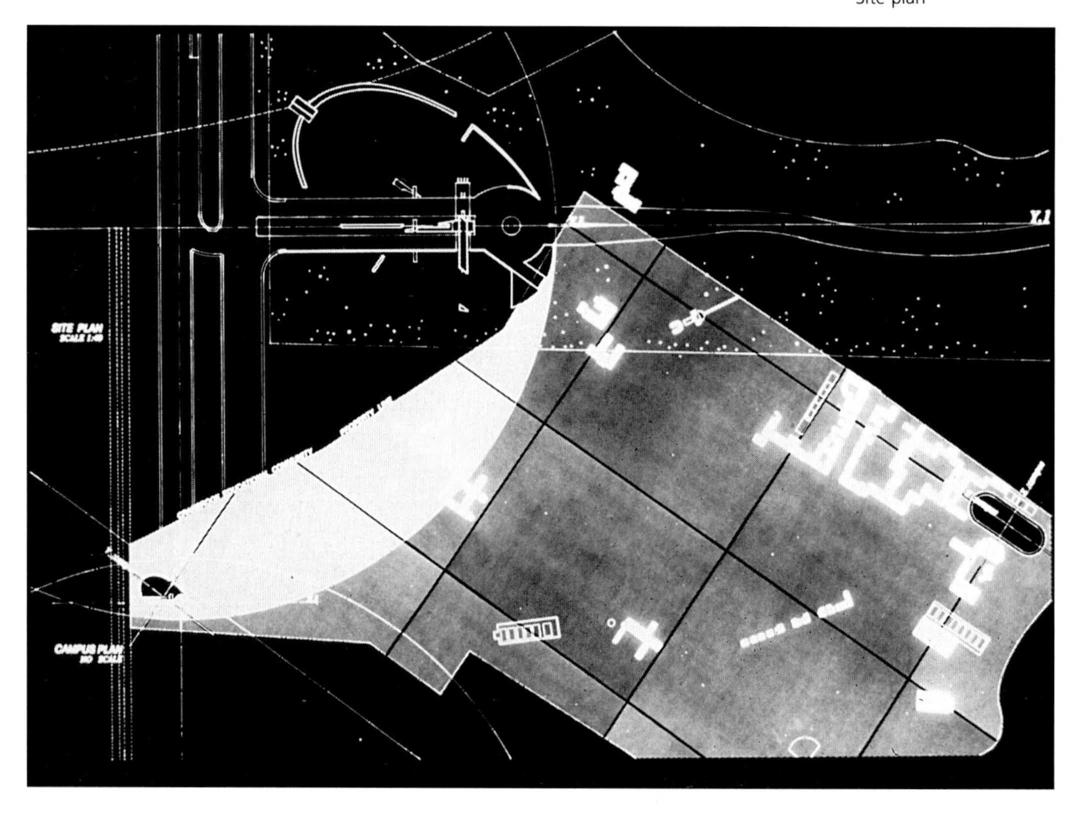

2
Cranbrook Gatehouse Competition, 1992
Project architect: Craig Burdick
Site plan

3
Cranbrook Gatehouse
Competition, 1992
Model

pass the Gatehouse at its end on a course which is centered within the space and which has a downward slope, reversing the perceptual experience upon entry and completing the access/egress cycle.

Reflecting an Abstract/Organizational Method

The work is a manifestation of an organizational strategy capable of representing a high degree of differentiation within a framework of order and continuity. The complex of elements expresses states of both harmony and tension – tension in the sense that the coexistence (between the willful architectural elements and augmented landscape) is inherently conflictive. Architectural-landscape elements confront, but are simultaneously at home with, the *more natural* nature. The fractured characteristic of the solutions provides a perpetual open endedness and unfinished quality to the projects. It is part of an accretive *making process* that anticipates the next intervention. The end of our work is the beginning for the community.

Many of these aspirations are embodied within the Blades Project. However, with this project our focus is on the domestication of space within nature. The work constructs boundaries that begin to wrest place from space – not to control nature, but to define a relationship of balance. A large exterior *room* has been created which forms a boundary or edge of habitation. This space embraces an augmented natural landscape and the

4
Blades Residence, Santa Barbara, California, 1992
Project architects: Kim Groves, Mark McVay
Model

main body of the construction, conveying a sense of sanctuary. Experientially, this reshaping strategy provides an opportunity for the occupant to witness the interactions of nature. One is made aware of the value of relationships, integration, and apparent haphazardness. Through the fusion of the exterior and interior worlds, the individual gradually becomes more oriented – learns to keep balance, bridging the gap between the subjective experience of our inner world and the objective experience of our external world.

The building arrangement, while reiterating the specific characteristics of this site, ultimately demonstrates its tentativeness to fixity by making overt reference to our temporary status as occupants.

Isolated Events within a Controlled Field

The Cranbrook and Blades investigations were situated within a suburban/rural context. Each in its way attempted to challenge the traditional dominance of the man-made object in favor of a more dispersed, fragmentary, and integrated relationship of our built environment and its site.

The Yuzen Automobile Museum and the Nara Convention Center, both addressing urban site situations, adhere to organizational methods which are attempting to appropriate and express specific events formed by the interrelationship of the program and the demands of the immediate context. The Yuzen Automobile Museum utilizes this strategy to make "adjustments" in scale and to find a language which addresses the automobile (what better place than Sunset Boulevard, L. A.?). Our competition entry in Nara differentiates a neutral site, providing a framework for future peripheral development by reshaping the ground surface (objects and spaces), reflecting the seventh century's influence on the city that we find today.

Of the two overriding concerns that governed the Yuzen Automobile Museum from its earliest conception, one is more pragmatic and the other conceptual. The first is an interest in confronting the site's commercial

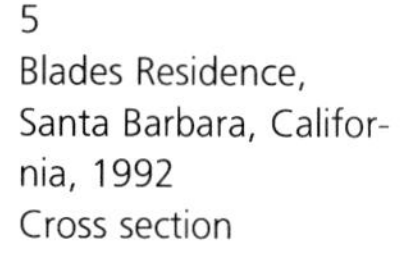

5
Blades Residence, Santa Barbara, California, 1992
Cross section

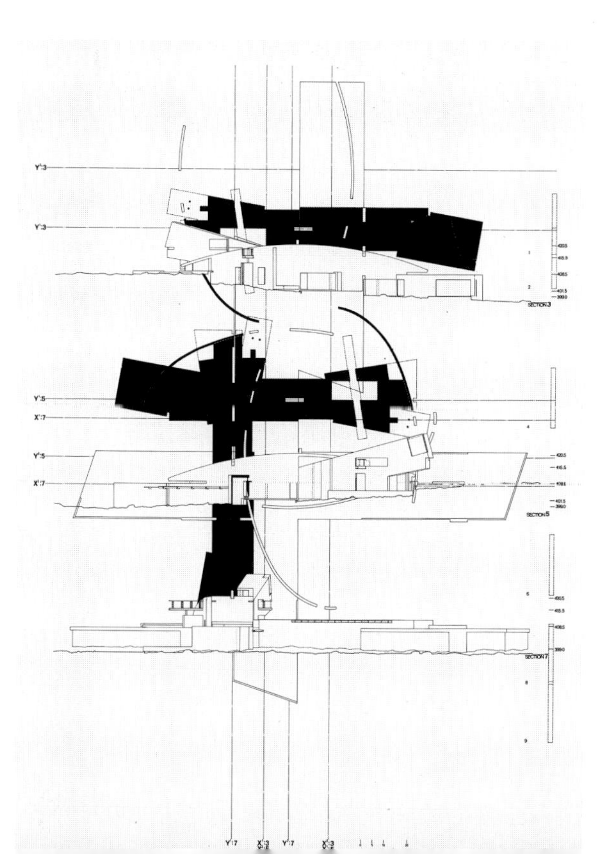

main street orientation to the north and the residential environment at its southern boundary. Our work attempts to resolve the visual impact of the buildings' massing, through the use of a ground (hugging) roof structure which itself becomes the new site for three building objects (restaurant, elevator/tower, and housing). A structural grid, an automobile car circulation system, and a peripheral edge-defining wall, make up the three primary orders that begin to formulate an architecture.

One's first glimpse of the Nara Convention Center from a vantage point at the railway station allows for the comprehension of a series of autonomous objects. Predominant from this view, and understood as the primary point of entry, is a kinetic interplay between the raised, transparent structure (the Black Box Theater) and the translucent wall against which it is silhouetted. The translucent quality will reveal an ever-changing dance of lights, people (actors and audience), and props in the small theater (as symbolic of the entire complex), while simultaneously providing a backdrop for projected images of contemporaneous events on the wall which runs the entire length of the site. At the other end of the site looms an egg-shaped volume differentiated from the diverse day-to-day

6
Yuzen Vintage Car Museum, Los Angeles, California, 1992
Project architect: John Enright
Project team: Craig Burdick, Kim Groves, Selwyn Ting, Michael Volk
Model

7
Nara Convention Center, Nara, Japan, 1992
Plans, cross sections

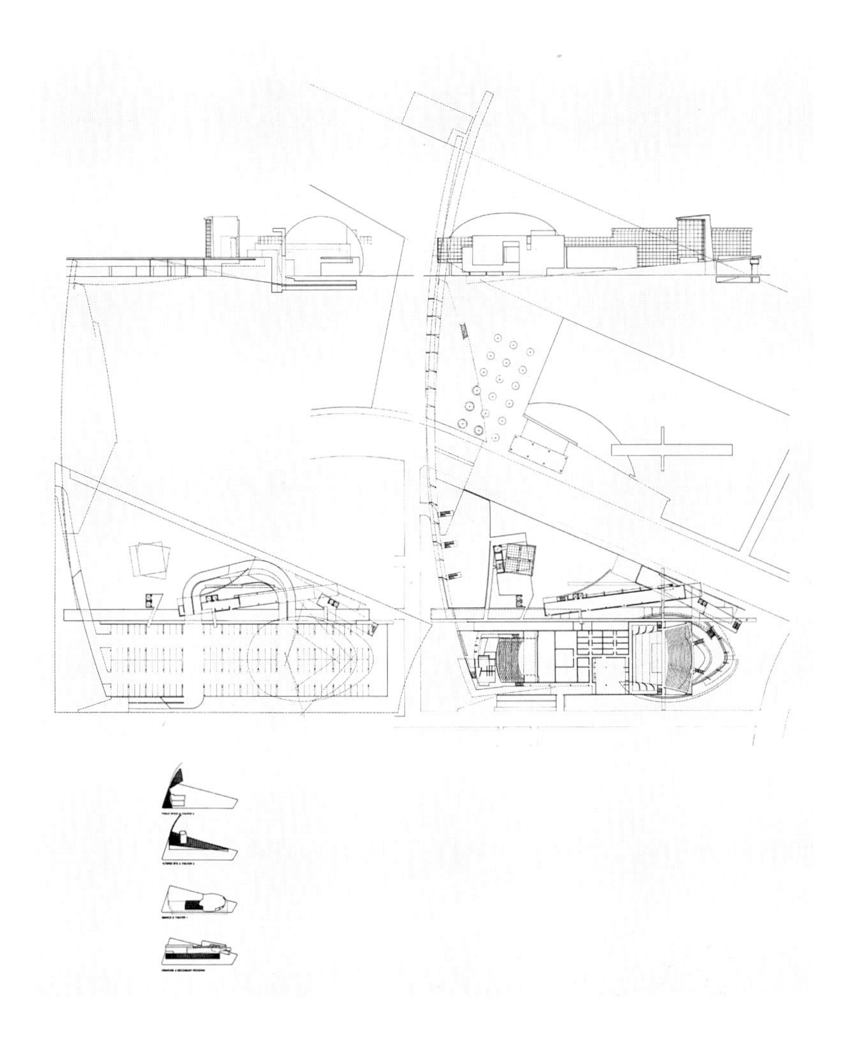

texture of the city. In contrast to the openness of the Black Box, this massive form – opaque, polished, and enigmatic – conceals its interior world. One can sense that these are but the beginnings in a series of more complex organizations. The egg as metaphor is enclosed, internal, and mysterious, yet evocative of the sublime beauty to be found in one of nature's most fundamental objects. It is meant as a comment on the city of Nara's historically central role in shaping the Japanese "mind," and serves as the *embryonic* point of departure for the future Redevelopment Project.

Our proposal responds to the contingent nature of these conditions by ordering the project into three imposed zone configurations. A sloping plane, evocative of the first amphitheaters, reconfigures the earth's surface in a gesture which produces a connecting figure bridging the "demilitarized zone" of the railroad with the station and the city center. This landscape procedure produces a boundary at the north. Pedestrians (both project- and city-bound) move on this plane to the Japan Railroad Station. At an urban level, this lifted plane metaphorically functions as a stage for the sculptural object which is, in fact, the Black Box Theater.

The urban character and the intensification of building mass of the second zone provides a contrast, and thus a balance to the naturalness and openness of the first. The site is axial and peripheral to the western boundary and produces the background and holding functions of the total complex. The large proscenium hall occupies its southern edge and prioritizes its position in a complex intersection by its dominance of scale and form. The middle portion of this area is lower in height and contains an interior park which serves to maintain the diversity of scale we so value as part of the heterogeneity of this city.

8
Nara Convention Center, Nara, Japan, 1992
Perspective view

9
Nara Convention Center, Nara, Japan, 1992
Perspective view

The third site is a triangular piece of land which is "given back to the city" and hence belongs to the existing community. The facade of the music hall lies on the edge of this triangle, providing a threshold or transition between the project and the grid of the city. There is a subterranean linkage to the station plaza at this edge of the site which provides a second connection vis à vis a sloped plaza which travels beneath the road. By working parallel to the bridge above, this linkage creates a strong sense of passage from the city to the complex. A series of public activities are envisioned to occupy and activate this space.

These three zones intensify and provoke a diverse set of urban experiences which enhance interrelationships while maintaining aspects of antonomy. The connective gesture which synthesizes these site-specific zones is a *slor* or deep street, cutting through the site on a direct north/south axis across and along which pedestrian movement occurs between the various programmatic elements of the total complex. The location of the three theaters, their related support facilities and the remaining functions of gallery, administration, and restaurants are a direct response to this site strategy and participate in a complex pedestrian movement system linking the three autonomous theaters.

The Nara complex, like the Yuzen museum project, oscillates between reaffirming the value of its place and confronting or reinterpreting this condition.

Eric Owen Moss

Out of Place Is the One Right Place

Moss Herbert, *Small Immensities.*

1
Westen Lawson House,
West Los Angeles,
California, 1993

In America there's an organization called the Sierra Club. Its members run around protecting the earth from a few obstreperous inhabitants. But they've got the wrong villains. As anyone who has mowed a lawn knows, the earth eats everything we put down on it – in perpetuity.

One:
The road is better than the inn.
Two: There is no inn.
Three: And no out.
Four: And no road.

Architecture is a fight against the Sierra Club; a fight against the perpetual eating machine; a fight against nihilism. Architecture is a sign to the next guy – the one who isn't born yet. So architecture isn't art or shelter or progress or the form of cities. It's the first sign on the road from nothingness. The act of doing the architecture, the primordial act, contests nihilism. That act precedes and supersedes all subsequent readings.

These are the steeds of Mars: Phobos and Demos – not what the National Aeronautics and Space Administration predicted. They're supposed to be spherical – they're not; and Phobos rotates retrograde, that is, in the wrong direction, assuming NASA knows the right direction. Science finds rules, chronology, sequence – predictability. The scientist's format is an *a priori* wish for comfort. And science gets a disingenuous, pre-determined teleology as a result. Look at the profile of Phobos. Whose computer did that come out of?

Milky
has no
weigh.

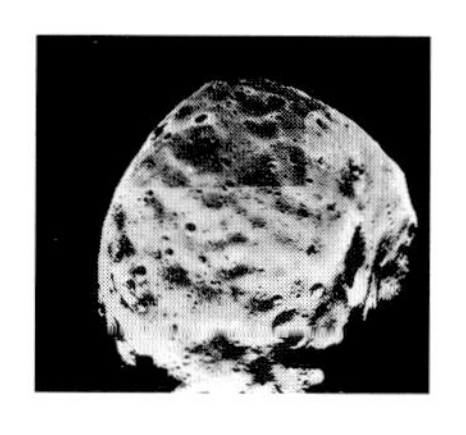

Architecture can deliver the mix – a need to comprehend, and the inability to comprehend. That's architecture's job at the end of the twentieth century.

Whatever comes
apart
Comes to get her.

This is the Caracol, the only helical building in the Yucatan. Caracol means snail. Nobody knows what it was; nobody knows what it did. Contemporary Mayans claim it was designed to chase the morning star, Venus. Maybe. A building that invented meaning on the ground by surveying the sky. NASA's still trying to do that.

Mayans saw differently; understood differently. The world they're trying to decipher is enigmatic. The Caracol is symmetrical and asymmetrical; it's quizzical. But the building embodies a societal consensus we don't possess. The snail unites architects and inhabitants of Chichenitza – all convinced of the merits of the Venus chase. The building mediates between society and the sky.

Experience says
no
To what it doesn't
know.

In the Mayan world, let's guess, meaning is extroverted, shared. There are no collective prospects today. Meaning is private. Is that a non sequitur?

One more thing. The Yucatan is a productive reference. It gets you outside the conventional Western lineage of architectural debate, gets you outside to go inside ...

Get rid of your
history
Or your history
gets rid of
you.

The burgeoning grid, appearing in Ohio museums, at military installations in Miletus, new towns in Britain, on structural plans in Berlin, and Park Avenue curtain walls. How to draw intelligible boundaries on an impervious planet? Ditto the plains of Nazga in the Peruvian highlands.

Crumpled Angor Wat. Probably not the way the builders expected to be remembered. Mr. Augustine has a teleological theory of history – history goes somewhere; it's directional. Ditto Aquinas, Marx, Toynbee. The gods of Angor Wat disagree. It feels like they're right. Looking into never ... Mies will be eaten too.

So where does one locate a reference, watching the coming and going of all references? Can architecture pontificate? Is architecture didactic? Yes and no, simultaneously. Schizophrenia is a cure, not a disease.

Measuring
yesterday
assumes
tomorrow.

So ... creation is an out-patient search. It's about time someone corrected Le Corbusier's drawing. Apollo – intellect, analysis, sequence, chronology, order; the measured; the understood; the ruled; the finite; the surface. And Dionysus – the raw material; under the understood; the unruled; the infinite; the depth. Apollo – xerox-reduced – tiny Apollo floats in a dubious boat on the Dionysian sea. Architecture can deliver that.

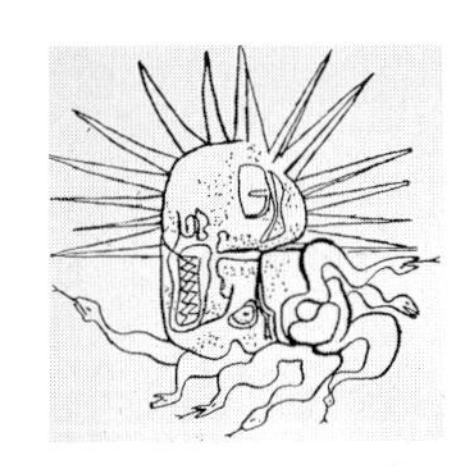

Find the
measure
measure
can't measure.

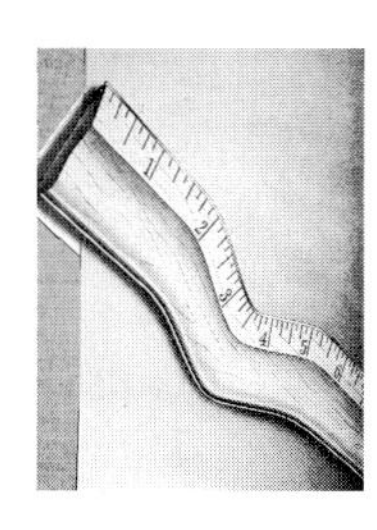

Is life four hands high? There's a need to quantify experience, to put a scale on the existential. But the biggest hole is dimensionless. Measure is a way to predict, like a clock. But everywhere you go it's a different time. So what time is it really?

Measure an area. Any area. Claim measure is its exegesis. But there's measure measure can't measure. Therefore bend your scale.

I'm not advocating. The rock-building is a conceivable hypothesis. Consider it. It's defensible as an option, as a place to begin. Any place is a place to begin. Funny? That's Lear's fool laughing. To attack today you have to invent a new weapon, today. Invent. Attack.

As you make
something you
know
Make
something
you don't know.

The ubiquitous machine, an omnipresence in architectural debate. Thomas Wolf once referred to the "beauty of the railroad car." The railroad car – that's the machine I'm interested in. Sometimes it works, sometimes it breaks (like Jimmy Carter's helicopters in the Iranian desert). It gets messy, dirty, greasy. It's erogenous. It's not confirmed by utility. It's not an idol, not a deity (like Lloyd's or the Hong Kong Bank). It's both asset and liability simultaneously, so it fits us. It's tactile. You can bite it. Hedonism. It can't be slick, quick and polished. And it's not a solution. It's a solution and a problem. But it's not pre-fab and off-the-shelf. It adds to a provisional vocabulary in architecture. It doesn't make the world better; it makes the world worse and better. It's not a progressive force, but it has increased the possibilities – the vulnerable machine, the confounding machine, the ubiquitous machine.

Schizophrenia
is a cure,
Not a
disease.

Ise – a seventh-century Taoist Shrine – embodies an eternal architectural dilemma: deliver both stillness and movement. Maybe the problem never changes, but the form of the answer has to.

The Shrine is constructed and stands for twenty years. Then it's dismantled and reconstructed on the adjacent site. It stands for twenty years. And is again disassembled and reassembled and so on ...

There's an
over
underneath
understand.

So the experience is constant and constantly changing. It's static, stable, durable, and fluid, evolving, deteriorating. Doom and renewal, finite and infinite. Truth in opposition, beauty through contradiction. But these guys are cheating. They appealed to an *a priori* belief system.

Surprise
is no
surprise.

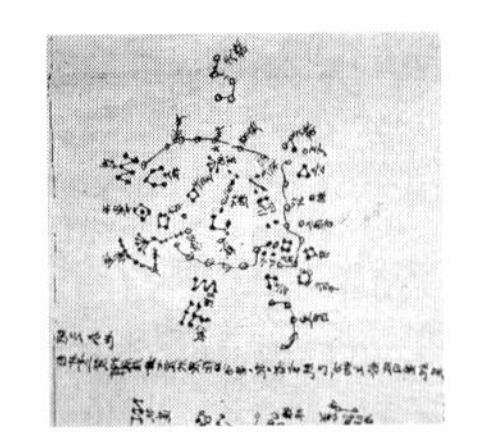

Where do we find still and still moving?

A Babylonian map of the sky. Four thousand years old. Why map the sky physically? To map the land emotionally. Chronicle the past; get it organized: the stars did this, the planets that. If the past is known, so the future. This is a map that tells you where you were and are and will be (it hopes). It locates you in time (maybe). With a map you can't get lost . . . or can you? The Babylonian map is out of date. Ours too. The ordering system in the sky and the *quid pro quo* on earth is a perpetual remodel.

How to know your location? At NASA they claim we've got the truth. Only a few details remain to be resolved. The priesthood always says that. Just like the Babylonians.

Running away
is running
towards
any way.

This is Los Angeles, another broken city. Everything moves, sometimes violently, sometimes imperceptibly. Moves outside; moves in your head. Even Abu Simbel.

The job is to look straight at it. Put down what you see. Don't run. Anyway, where would you go . . . at the end of the twentieth.

Moss Herbert, *Small Immensities.*

No Irreversible Solutions: You Lose and Retrieve Good Moments

You start to get suspicious at an early point about whether anyone knows what the hell they're talking about. Suspicious of yourself, too.

You can't work with ideas that have lost their vitality. You have to transplant the heart or reinvigorate the blood . . . But you can't keep using and re-using language which is dead.

From *Zarathustra* on the subject of old and new: "Here do I sit and wait, all the old tables busted, no good. No new tables." I think what post-moderns do is to edit the old tables. And I'm saying the tables are irreparable.

You have to be careful, finally, that somebody who has discovered something which comes to be prized is not allowed to discover anything else, because the people who value the first discovery are coming to buy.

In fact, there are no clocks. I mean, if there were no people here . . . So that the sort of dissection

of life into something which is related to clock time is artifice. And I think that if a building gets you beyond clock time, it changes your frame of reference, because then you start to understand that being on schedule won't help you. So here's something else, and I'm going to give it to you. I'm making it available to you; if you want to pick it up, pick it up. But you can't put a watch on it.

What's very appealing about *The Trial* is that there's an impossible search for a narrative, for a rationale, for an explanation. And in the most profound, artistic way, frustratingly, it never exists! You never get it. Because it's not there. It's just not there ... and yet you've got to keep looking.

Wait a minute! This guy Kafka is one of the most peculiar people imaginable. His insights and his sensibilities are unique. And he relies on those. And the reason he relies on those is because there's nothing else. He puts something down, and very strangely, it registers with lots of people. They understand exactly what he's talking about.

Pascal once said that life was a line of people marching to the guillotine. Marching irrevocably. And the only thing you could do was jump out of line, run to the front, and stick your head under the blade. Architecture can make that run. Painting, too. Remember *Saturn Devouring His Children*?

Can you imagine the son-of-a-bitch who tried to draw a map of *Finnegan's Wake* ...? But that's part of the aspiration to pin things down.

The problem for me is to learn how to be comfortable being uncomfortable. I don't think, when you translate that into architecture, it means people have to walk on their hands. Maybe comfort has to do with knowing the circumstances *a priori*; knowing where you're going before you get there. And I think what I would like very much is for someone to come into these buildings, year after year, and to think, "This is the first time I've been here."

We have to be very careful not to look for tricks or events or games. I think we're looking for a kind of investigation which is longer-running, deeper, and more precarious. In a certain sense, the process must defy a coherent or single explanation – and yet don't you feel everything is a game sometimes? And that you can't get outside the game?

I like the back room because I think it's one of the few cases (and I don't think you do it too often) where I actually hit what I was after. It slips away. Then you start to get your hands on it a little bit, and then it dissipates again. You can't lock it up. It's too elusive. Architecture is grabbing chocolate pudding.

2
Gary Group, Culver City, California, 1988–90
Facade

3
Hayden Bridge, S.P.A.R.CITY, Culver City, California, 1991

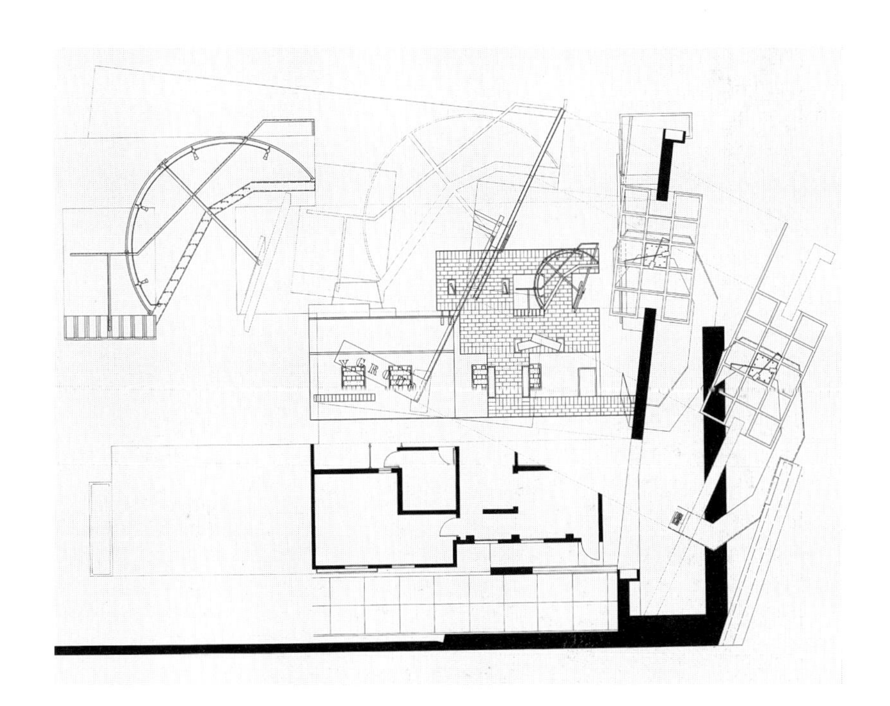

4
Gary Group, Culver City, California, 1988–90
Elevation

5
Gary Group, Culver City, California, 1988–90
Conference room

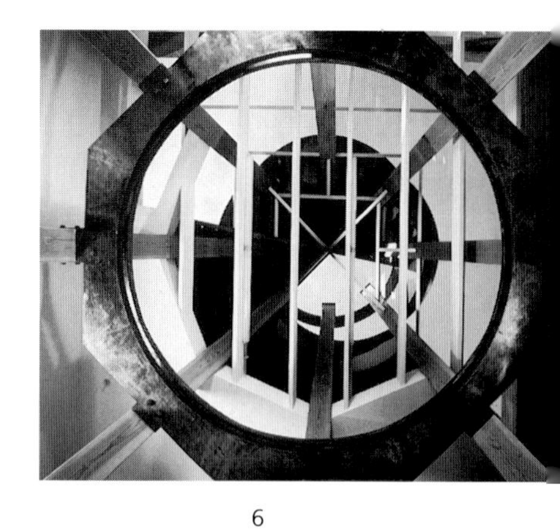

6
Gary Group, Culver City, California, 1988–90
Looking up from the conference room

7
National Boulevard, Culver City, California, 1986–90
Office

8
National Boulevard,
Culver City, California,
1986–90
Staircase

9
National Boulevard,
Culver City, California,
1986–90
Conference room

10
P & D Guest House,
Los Angeles, California,
1992

11
Rhino Records Head-
quarters, Culver City,
California, 1993

12
Samitaur Offices, Los
Angeles, California,
1993

13
Nara Convention Center, Nara, Japan, 1991
Model

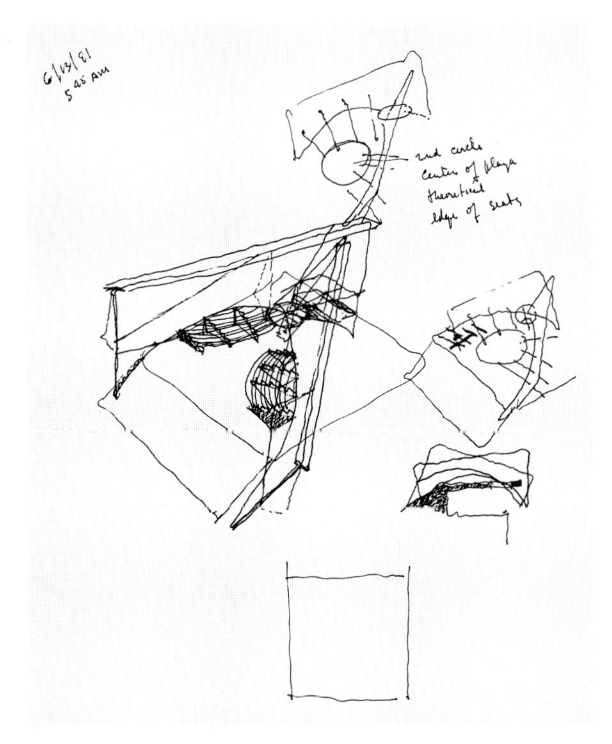

14
Terrace of the MAK-Austrian Museum of Fine Arts, Vienna
Sketch

Carme Pinós

Following the Trace

I do not wish to hear speak of that which is new, of that which is different, as these words do not interest me. I am only interested in that which is original, "original" in the sense of origin, of re-establishment, of beginning again, of going to the source, which implies the existence of something incontrovertible. This, to me, is the complete opposite of the negation of significance. It is in the "significant" that resides all of the strings that are there to be pulled. Like the composer who sat down and played a second time when he was asked for an explanation of his complex study, I will explain my approach by explaining my work.

I will begin by speaking of the cemetery in Igualada. The words "place," "presence," and "silence" are those which occur to me when asked to explain our project. We immersed ourselves in the place, bathed in it, and felt its presence. The emphasis of this presence is our project; we descended more into the presence of the place. For this we sought silence; the material uniformity blurred the limits of our actions; diluting them in the earth helped us find it.

There was place as topography, as landscape, but place also understood in terms of everyday culture. We have made the Sunday stroll to the cemetery, our project.

From the fluidity embodied in our vision of life – a word both present and absent in a cemetery – we availed ourselves of the opportunity to design the pavement.

We have placed trees in the entrance of the cemetery, because they speak to us of the passing of time; flowering in spring, fruiting in summer, and leafless in winter. We have filled the cemetery with the significances that we encounter in our culture. We have tried to be another link, but an original link, with our tradition. "Aesthetic inventions are archaic, carrying within them the impulse of a distant source" (George Steiner).

The project in Hostalets was also realized with Enric Miralles. Here, the brief was to make the place one of games, of encounters. The whole building had to be walkable, palpable – it is place itself. Here, we made a mountain to climb, just as previously in the cemetery we descended. From above, from the terrace, it is possible to watch the games that go on in the garden, while at the same time we can see the neighboring mountains.

1
Igualada Cemetery, Poligono Industrial Igualada, 1985
Architects: Carme Pinós, Enric Miralles
Project team: Se Duch, Albert Ferre, Eva Prats

To our pleasant surprise, a mountaineering club has availed itself of the multi-use space, and they climb the roof and walls. We could not have asked for anything better!

The main hall presents a large illuminated window to the main street of the town, along which holiday-makers stroll. We wanted the town to be known not only for its church or town hall, but also for our large window. We immersed ourselves as much as possible in the place where we were working, with the people who were going to use the building; we made them ascend, look from on high, walk towards the large illuminated window.

2, 3
Igualada Cemetery,
Poligono Industrial
Igualada, 1985

4–6
Civic Center, Hostalets de Balenya, Barcelona, 1986–92
Project team: Se Duch, Albert Ferre, Eva Prats

In the next three projects (realized without Enric Miralles), the brief was almost exclusively to resolve a place of conflict, the wreckage of unrelated actions. My response was to immerse myself in the conflict, whereas before I had immersed myself in the place.

The first project is for a promenade in a coastal town under great pressure from tourism. The conflict between the growth of the city towards the sea and the refusal of the beach to be constrained is materialized in a line which characterizes the beach as an artificial landscape, a

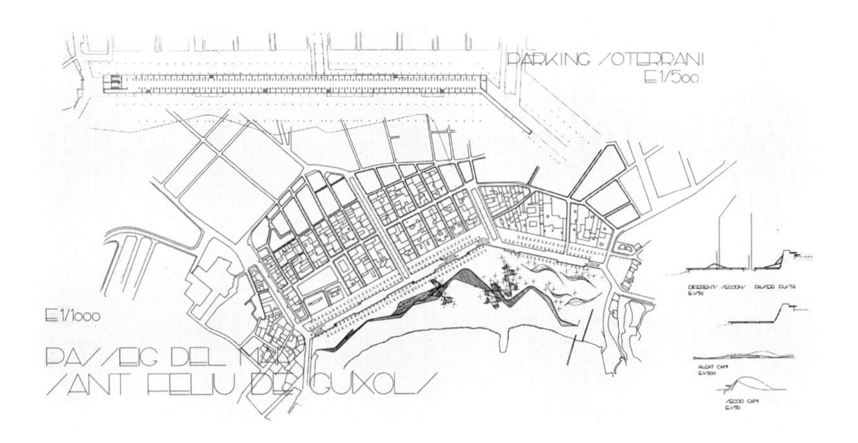

7, 8
Sant Feliu de Guixols
Plan; model

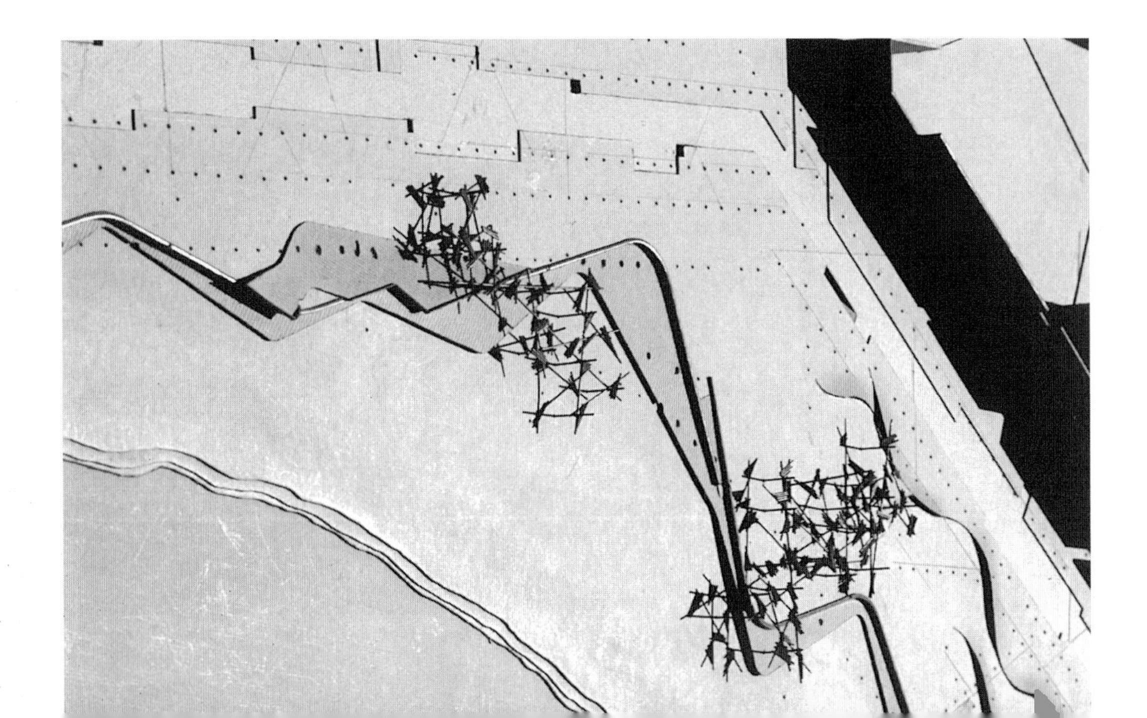

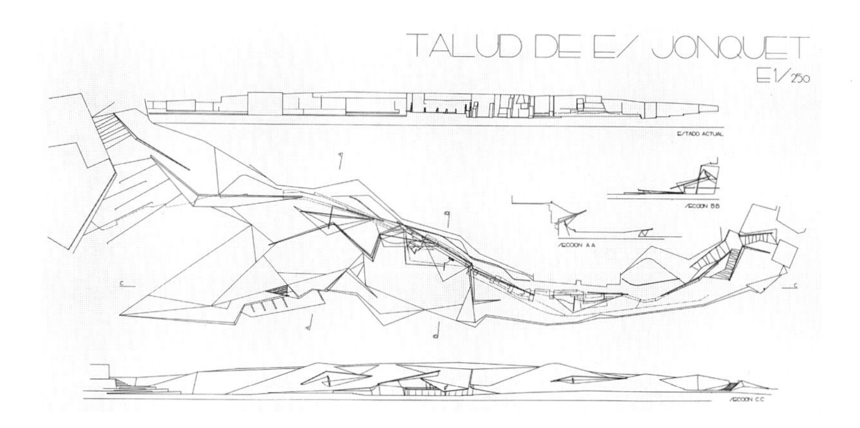

9, 10
Talud de es Jonquet,
Palma de Mallorca,
1992
Model; plan

point of encounter between the opposing forces. The pergolas, corralling the trees that jump between them, go down to the water's edge, reconciling themselves with the virgin landscape which has already disappeared.

A low concrete retaining wall delineates the beach and the urban park. A timber pavement over the sand, the last vestige of civilization, will be the place where, in winter, when people do not wish to stroll on the sand, they will walk with thoughts of the city far away. The path of this wall provides places and corners to be discovered, as in any landscape. The beach ceases to be just square meters of towel-park.

The next project is situated in the city of Palma de Mallorca. A concrete retaining wall has replaced the original cliffs, above which is located the old fishermen's quarter. The continual expropriation of the cliffs to

11, 12
Talud de es Jonquet, Palma de Mallorca, 1992
View of the city with supporting wall and model of the new fortifications

provide more space for the city had endangered the very existence of the "barrio," and the whole embankment had to be faced in concrete. The city council has stopped all further development, leaving a small lot, closed on one side by the retaining wall and on the other by the coastal highway. The brief was to improve the retaining wall, which did not enhance the image of the city.

My project was to make a vertical garden. The concrete that formed the retaining wall now forms more horizontal platforms that contain the earth I let fall from above: what was a vertical and hostile wall has now become horizontal and shelters me.

Then, seeing a garden as an artificial landscape, I wanted to form a sketch with concrete and earth – which for me are grey and green, too – in which we recognize nothing. The sketch begins above at the edge of the barrio and finishes at the edge of the highway; like playing with a sheet of paper with irregular cuts, it has various layers, one part pulled up and the other part down. The spaces – squares, benches, paths – are recognized when we enter the drawing, not due to their proximity but because we find ourselves using them.

My intention was not to return to the character of the natural cliff, but to reconcile the aggression implicit in the subjection of nature by the concrete, and the necessity to surround ourselves with it.

The project at Mont-Saint-Michel had to harmonize many different things: tourism, cars, a historical monument, a virgin landscape reclaimed from the sea, an extraordinary vacuum, and the insularity of the island itself.

13
Mont-Saint-Michel,
Project, 1991
View and plan of
Mont-Saint-Michel with
sections

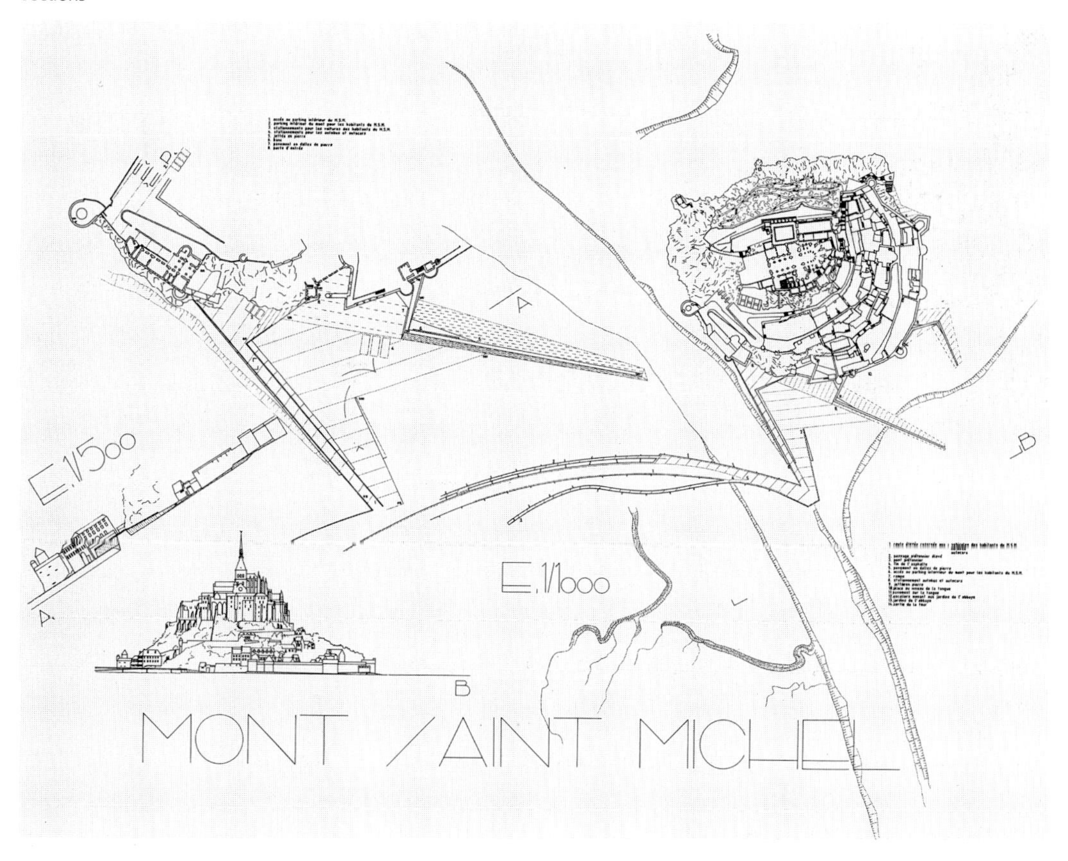

In preliminary meetings everybody was objecting: they argued about cars, about tourists – even about the reclaimed land (the "herbus"), which I found amazing. This is land with which nothing can be done, because from time to time it is completely covered by the sea; then Mont-Saint-Michel appears as something distant, a reminder of the untouchable act of nature that continues to protect it.

My project, or rather proposal, intends to give substance to the elements that are considered problematic by turning each of the problems on its head. If parked cars are thought an annoyance, then I will value the shine of their bonnets seen from the Mount, and I will make a sketch of that which I am happy to contemplate from afar.

I will accept that tourism is the only reality of Mont-Saint-Michel. An ancient place of pilgrimage, later a prison, and now a historical monument, the Mount has always had an isolated character. Since tourism is "an escape from everyday life," a search for places and architectures evoking lifestyles totally distinct from our own, then I will endeavor to return this isolated character, this faraway presence. It is from the "herbus" that this presence is seen best. I wish to arrive at Mont-Saint-Michel imperceptibly, almost without leaving a trace.

I imagine that I rise above the river in a car in order to see the Mount from on high, and after that, I glide over the "herbus" almost without touching it. For this reason the road will be made of pieces of encrusted, separated concrete blocks, which will support the weight of a car but will not permit great speed. Grass will grow in the spaces. Small raised embankments manipulate the view of the Mount, allowing it to appear and disappear: I attempt to control the view as a director controls a film. Arrival is by way of a curved bridge, from behind; from the car, you always see the sea between you and the Mount.

I have also tried to create a recognizable horizon. The structure of the bridge is a repetition of the first bridge over the river, already far away. First, the horizon was created on the causeway that penetrates the sea, and now on the bridge that brings you to the Mount.

This last bridge is interrupted by the car park. A large mound of earth shuts off the view, which is recaptured when you climb it to find a parking space in its folds. Lines of trees accompany you on the descent, gracing the vision of the Mount. Everything contributes to make this vision a *mise en scène* which will last a day or, if you are only passing, for a few hours. If you should wish to stay, you leave the car inside the town, taking advantage of the existing carriage gate. So that visitors do not feel imprisoned by the city walls, stone breakwaters form a small square on the other side of them allowing people to stroll on the wet sand surrounding Mont-Saint-Michel.

My final project is a unique action, and I trust that its resonances have formed the whole environment. The commission was to design a walkway that would unite a small suburb with the town of Petrer; the existing link goes alongside a Gothic aqueduct.

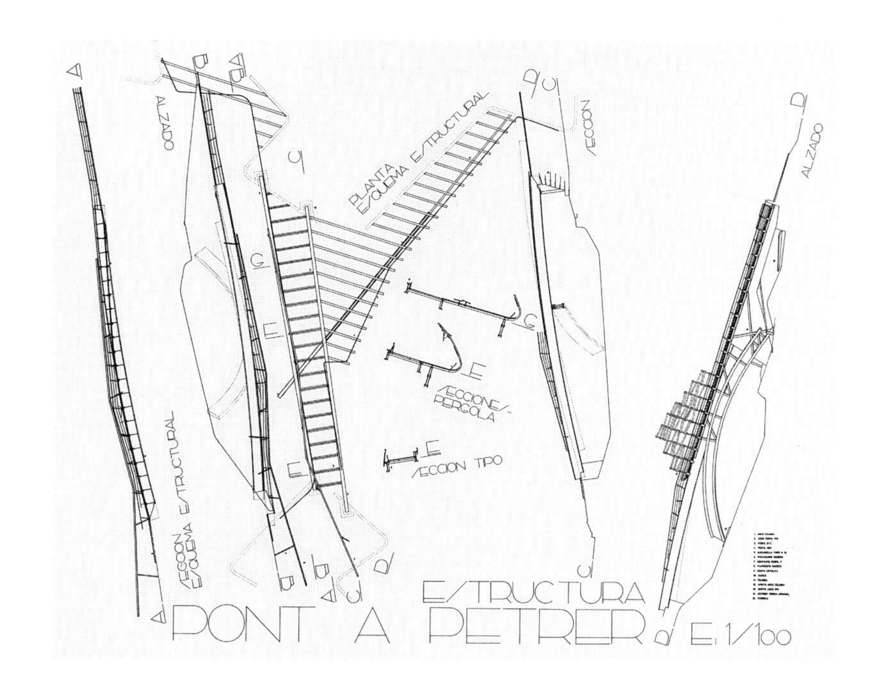

14, 15
Path and bridge at
Petrer, 1991
Plan; model

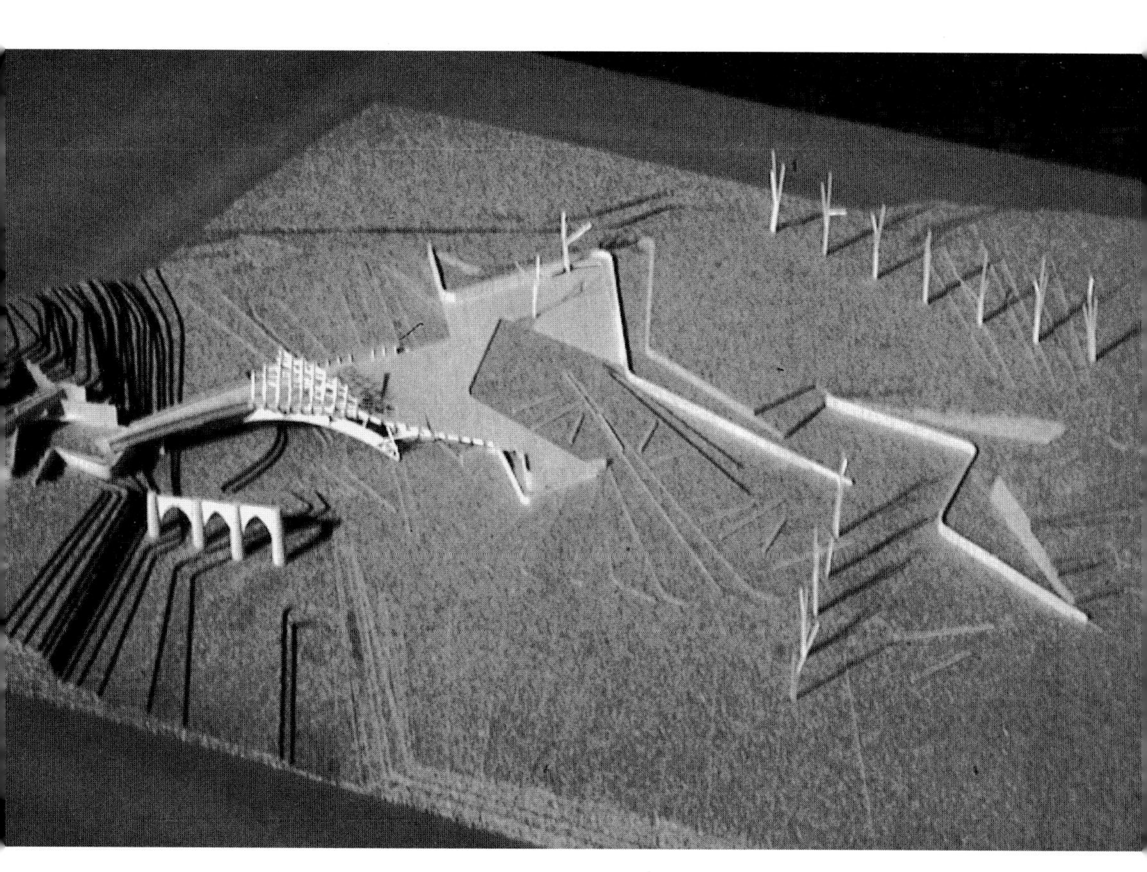

16
Path and bridge at
Petrer, 1991
Model

17
Path and bridge at
Petrer, 1991
Model of the bridge

Rather than create a directional walkway, my intention is to make a more static space: a third arch crosses the two that form the walkway, to create a square. The pavement is extended further than the bridge, provoking a remodulation of the landscape. The aqueduct will be a monument, presiding over the square. The beams that support the walkway oversail and fold to form a pergola.

From the bridge in the square we can contemplate the landscape, defined by two "parterres" that follow the movement of the ground – one closing the square, the other delineating the path.

I have tried, within a very tight budget and with a very simple project, to provide the suburb with the urban space that it lacked, and to convert what is now an arid landscape into something that could be described as a garden.

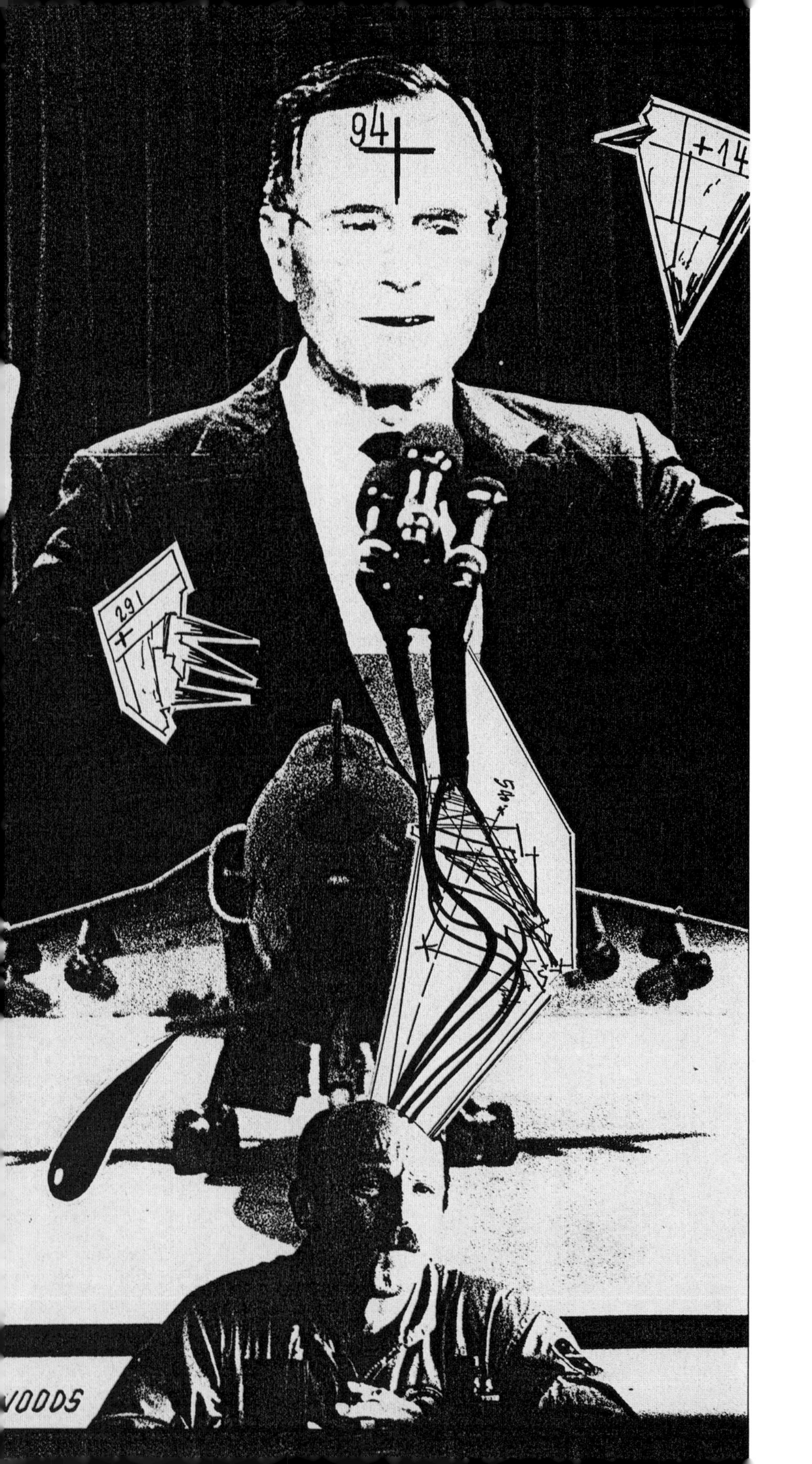
94
+14
291

Lebbeus Woods

Freespace and the Tyranny of Types

1
When the Brass Head Speaks

The war continues. It rages across an earth ruined by petty ambitions. Among these a brutal will to power cannot be found, only a will to succeed, to be accepted as an equal, therefore as a less-than-equal. The earth is ruined, and the subtle creatures crawling on it raise terrible sounds into the sky, cries and commands, arguments and excuses, pleadings for mercy, appeals for justice. But the buildings do not move.

The architect is in his room. From his window above (always above), he looks down on the fragile patterns of the city, on a landscape crawling with insects. For a moment he pretends he is one of them, then returns to his production machines. The walls that enclose his room were not built by him, but by nameless workers of an earlier epoch, clever worker insects, skilled insects, obedient insects. The walls tremble with their energy, which is somehow contained in the bricks, in the crumbling mortar. He hates these insect walls, and wants to tear them down with his bare hands. Instead, he designs new ones.

The new walls are of a new material, a nameless material. He must invent a name for them, and he does. They will be called architecture. The material of which they are made requires no workers, no energetic beetles, no skilled cockroaches.

2
Come the Revolution

Architecture has always served power and authority in society. It has always served wealth and the wealthy, and is sure to continue this role, by serving to monumentalize, mythologize, and confirm for the public the interests of the already powerful, thereby convincing the non-wealthy that the interests of the wealthy are their interests, too. Museums, funded by rich patrons, rich corporations, and rich governments, are especially effective in this selling of private interests in the name of public good. They purvey culture as a commodity available to anyone with the price of admission, measured not in the local currency, but in the currency of a desire to belong, to play the game.

1
Monument
From the Zagreb Free
Zone collages, 1991

D. H. Lawrence, in his *Apocalypse*, states the case with all the proto-Fascist lyricism of a latter-day Carlyle: *when we deny the hero, we deny ourselves*. The modern hero is sometimes a great leader, but more often someone who achieves wealth and power behind the scenes. Hence the allure of the Godfather. There is still, even in the public mind, a certain vulgarity associated with fame. In fact, the real price of fame is to remain second-rank, if not second-rate.

A comeuppance is often in store. The only thing more exhilarating than watching a star rise is watching the same star fall. The only unassailable modern heroes are those who appear in the firmament and remain there mysteriously, without fanfare or apparent effort: they are the true stars, the products of a cool, remote, steady, and higher sphere. "Being There" is how Jerzy Kosinsky put it in his fable of charismatic power. The true stars are (no surprise) the *aristoi*, the Immortals, the rich patrons, the patronizing corporations whose effortless support holds up the worlds of culture, art and architecture. I know of only one architect who fits into this category. The rest sweat too much.

But I foresee another kind of architect, another kind of architecture, with another role to perform within this same society already so effectively dominated by the rich and powerful. It is an architecture operating outside the game. Let me be clear on this point: it is not an architecture of revolution, for to revolt is to confirm the game – in fact, to play the game. The architecture I have in mind is simply outside the prevailing game of wealth, power, authority. It is its own game, has its own rules, its own means and ends. The material of which it is made, however, is the same history, the same present, the same potentiality as those of the *aristoi* and their willing public. If this other architecture threatens the prevailing one, all the better. Two birds with one stone. The architect I foresee is the *experimental* architect. His sweat is the color of blood.

2
Monument
From the Zagreb Free Zone collages, 1991

3
The Wrong Side of the Tracks

Some few hundred kilometers to the south of Vienna, war is being waged in the name of nationalism, which is a mask covering lust for wealth and greed for territory. It is a war which has destroyed the fabric of cities and towns, of economies, cultures, and lives. This war will continue, in one form or another, because no one with the power to stop it is willing to do so. That is an issue of human values, of strength of character, or the lack of it. And it will not be the last war, in Europe or elsewhere. The riots in Los Angeles in May 1992 are but one part of an ongoing rebellion in the USA, a rebellion against a social system constructed on greed and lust for wealth.

Whether or not those who violently rebel, or defend themselves against violent aggression by superior force, win their wars to preserve their identity and dignity – their freedom to be who they are – remains to be seen. The odds are heavily against them. The weight of powerful institutions is against them: in the case of Bosnia and Croatia, the Serbian armed forces and the paranoid leadership directing them; in the USA, corporations, governments, and the "silent majority" who believe they have everything to lose if the prevailing order is overturned, even though that order uses repressive violence to maintain itself.

Architects, who design the buildings symbolizing the prevailing authority in society, especially those architects who monumentalize authority by making its buildings into "art," are part of the repression, part of the weight against those who are today being crushed into submission by the most brutal means. No doubt these architects argue that their concern is architecture and not politics, not social conditions over which they might also claim they have no control. The best of these architects believe that they are serving the "higher interests" of civilization, those qualities of thought and action that transcend the passing problems of the world, that are the timeless ingredients of art and science. But what if civilization itself is changing, and with it the very nature of its higher interests? What if these higher interests, that the architect seeks to serve, no longer require transcending the turbulent changes of the present, but active engagement with them? In that case, the architects who monumentalize authority resisting change, authority that seeks to maintain itself as a status quo, are not today serving civilization, but its enemies: categorization, oversimplification, typology.

3
Dreadnought
From the Zagreb Free Zone collages, 1991

4
The Strange Case of Space Ex

Wherein the author attempts (a) to disclose an essential link between types of buildings currently commissioned for design and construction, and the prevailing system of ordering space for human habitation; (b) to state clearly that certain important building types are becoming obsolete, owing to profound changes in the philosophical, social and political conditions of living; (c) to call for the introduction of new building types, which shall be in effect building anti-types; (d) to conclude that architects are responsible for the introduction of these new anti-types, owing to their position in society as practitioners of a comprehensive art; (e) to assert that anti-types require new systems of ordering space.

(a) Building types correspond with economic categories, directly with lines in an accountant's ledger: *housing, office, utilities, shopping, medicine, manufacture*. These correspond, in turn, with the elements of Cartesian duality: God and mind are forever separate, incommutable. Spirit, if it exists at all, is not considered in mental frames, but is forever banished from its coordinates: x, y, z. Yet this triad refers equally to the Trinity as to Aristotelian logic. God, or as much of Him as we are able to know, is to be found in mathematics and music. The architecture of types, the degraded mathematics, the mathematics of the hand-worker and not the head-worker, follows only calculable Cartesian patterns and not the metaphysical matrices of Pythagoras, the *magus* and musician.

(b) But the magus-musician is important, because his metaphysics propose the non-linear complexity of rapidly changing conditions, which can only be a little bit predicted and even less controlled. He proposes to get into the flow, into the turbulence of change and somehow to draw from it elusive patterns and energies. This "somehow" is his magic. And is he not standing in for all those "somebodies" who must suffer change themselves, each in their own way and time? – those who must endure and forebear, who must, in other words, live by their wits, day to day – the citizens of Zagreb, Sarajevo, and Moscow, the citizens of Los Angeles, New York, Berlin, Tokyo.

Do not speak to them about building types, the categories of an order rendered ever more transparent by changes. They work in their homes, at computers or sewing machines. Their children are educated by television, in living rooms, or basements, or in the streets. The factory that they worked in yesterday is today a parking garage, a shopping mall, or a ruin. The once-plush office is now just unleased space. What these people want is the same thing the magus-musician wants: mobility, fluidity, poise, agility, the ability to draw strength from the turbulence of existence itself.

(c) Today, new conditions of living demand new types of space, new types of buildings which serve as instruments of turbulence, which simultaneously create and measure *particular* turbulences. Their particularity is not categorical, the usual Cartesian tyranny of types, but entirely phenomenological, entirely rooted in the phenomena of change. This condition reverses the normal duality of relationship, in which architecture is a generalized mathematical container with an elaborate description. In the new, turbulent condition, description is generalized, while architecture is highly articulated in material qualities.

This corresponds to the nature of changes occurring in modern conditions of existence, the epistemological shift from causal determinism to indeterminacy. Today, cause and effect are not seen to form a logical chain, but exist as parallel conditions in a fluctuating field of probabilities. Form and function cannot be linked by a verb, any more than architecture instrumental in change and any description of it can be linked to anything else by predetermined meaning. Today such architecture can only be described by anti-description. The building type becomes the anti-type. The building, in other words, becomes *atypical*, so highly particular in plastic terms that it can serve only as a model for itself. In a word, *freespace*.

(d) It is not the developer, the bureaucrat, the institutional client who is responsible for inventing freespace, but the architect. Only architecture – the act, the idea, the discipline – can "somehow" break limits and at the same time establish them. Only architecture can embody the irreducible paradox of at once both being and becoming, of being the result of x, y, and z and becoming something else – ineffable coordinates of mind which have no sign or significance at all, other than "free."

(e) Nearly a century ago, Albert Einstein said: "We know now that science cannot grow out of empiricism alone, that in the constructions of science we need to use free invention which only *a posteriori* can be confirmed with experience as to its usefulness. This fact could elude earlier generations, to whom theoretical creation seemed to grow inductively out of empiricism without the creative influence of a free construction of concepts. The more primitive the status of science is, the more readily can the scientist live under the illusion that he is a pure empiricist." In order to embody a new conception of "I" which the twentieth century, with its accelerated speeds and accelerated pace of change, demanded, Einstein had to invent a new, free construction of space and time in which the "I," the lone, existential observer, occupied the critical and crucial position. Then, in order to extend this construction to the human limits of space and time, he had to adopt a new, anti-Euclidean, anti-Cartesian geometry inscribing space and time.

The principal task of the experimental architect today is to inscribe space and time with the paradoxical dimensions of a relativistic "I" – the lone and abandoned citizen of a brutal New World, freed by no choice of his own, but, paradoxically, by the changing conditions in which his own condition is the cause of its crisis.

5
Manifesto

Architecture and war are not incompatible. Architecture is war. War is architecture.
I am at war with my time, with history, with all authority that resides in fixed and frightened forms.
I am one of millions who do not fit in, who have no home, no family, no doctrine, no firm place to call my own, no known beginning or end, no "sacred and primordial site."
I declare war on all icons and finalities, on all histories that would chain me with my own falseness, my own pitiful fears.
I know only moments, and lifetimes that are as moments, and forms that appear with infinite strength, then "melt into air."
I am an architect, a constructor of worlds, a sensualist who worships the flesh, the melody, a silhouette against the darkening sky. I cannot know your name. Nor can you know mine.
Tomorrow, we begin together the construction of a city.

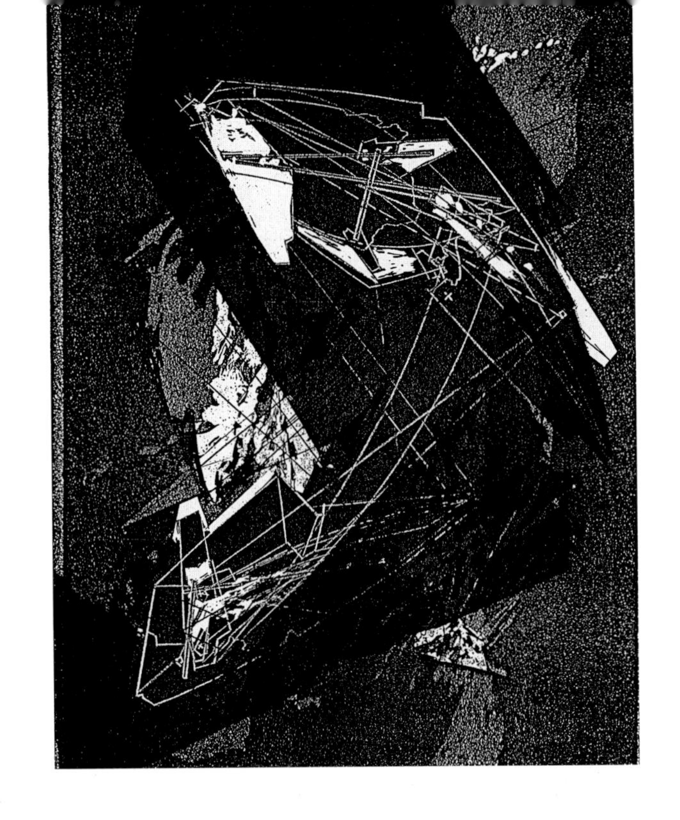

4, 5
Heterarchy
From the Free Zone
studies, 1991

6
Freespace Structure in Transit
From Zagreb Free Zone, 1991

7
Anti-Gravity House, 1992

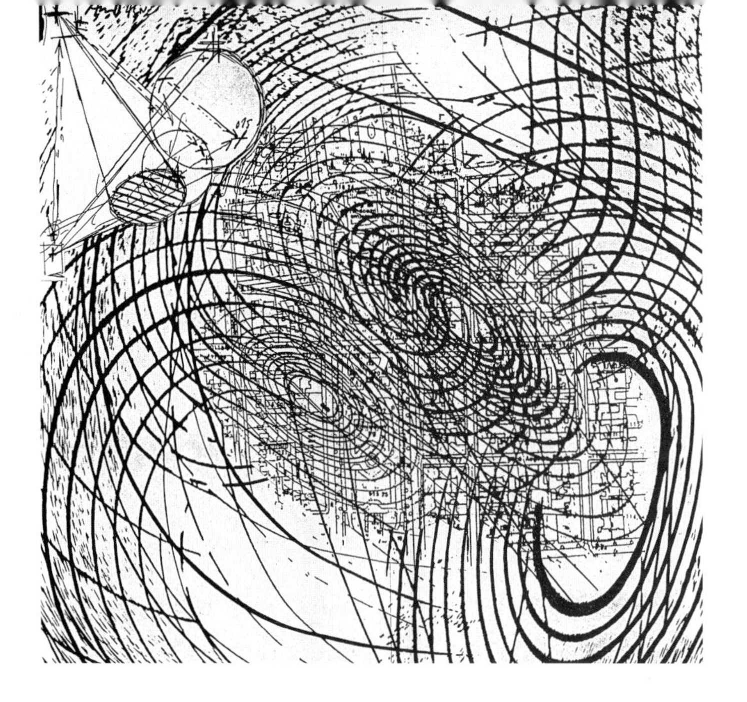

8
Electromagnetic Perturbations
From Zagreb Free Zone, 1991

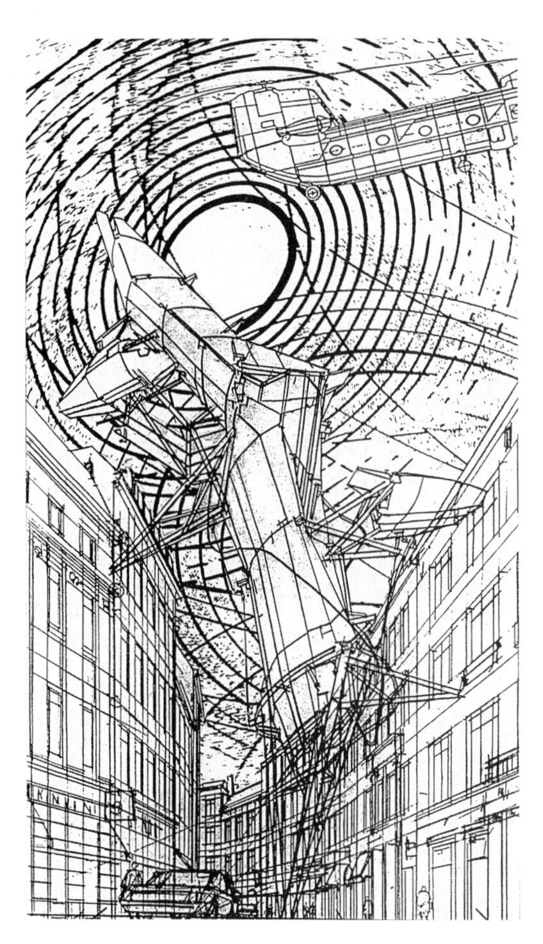

9
Freespace Structure in Place (suspended)
From Zagreb Free Zone, 1991

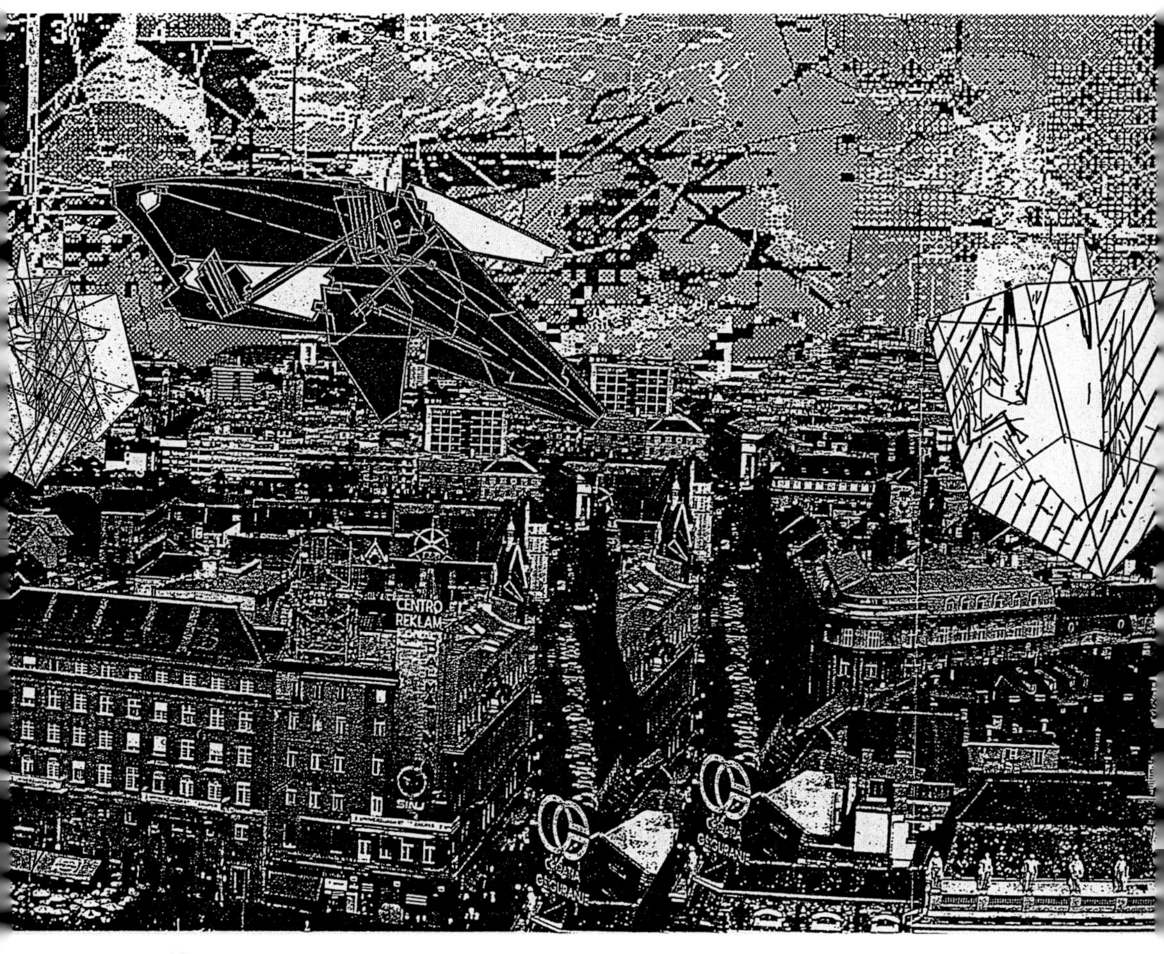

10
Free Zone Composite
From Zagreb Free Zone,
1991

Prologue

Clarity and authenticity were the primary objectives in the editing of the following discussion. Like many such roundtables, this conversation, too, was cyclical. For clarity, it has been broken into segments that address several recurrent themes; for the sake of authenticity, these segments are presented by and large in the sequence in which they occurred.

The conversation begins with a debate on attitudes to history, in which the "tabula rasa" approach is weighed against the lessons and polemical uses of historical precedent.

In the ensuing discussion, the need to define a collective agenda crops up repeatedly. In one respect, it can be read as a search for consensual parameters for architecture; in another sense, the discourse is engaged with finding credible ways to determine and serve the public interest. Certainly, the question of reinstating an underlying program for architecture is long overdue, but readers may be surprised to find it emerging so insistently from a group of architects most commonly associated with the pursuit of highly personal, "artistic" visions.

Naturally, questions of political and social relevance – and of power – enter into the proposition of an agenda. Coloring the conversation is this group's recognition that architecture is becoming increasingly marginal in the broader scheme of things, and their self-perception as a minority operating on the fringe of an already peripheral vocation.

Another related "cycle" in the roundtable deals with clients and program. United in opposition to the status quo, the conferees approach agreement on the need to liberate building programs from their functional and typological shackles. The question of "creating" new kinds of clients emerges as a corollary to the redefinition of program: the patronage to be encouraged, in this group's view, would be more inclined to support a public-spirited architecture focused on spatial experience, rather than predetermined by use or yield.

It would be too much to expect issues of such complexity to be resolved in one sitting. But as the first in what could evolve into a series of pan- and multidisciplinary meetings, this conference has great value for its timely confrontation of the questions.

Ziva Freiman
New York, October 1992

Vienna Architecture Conference June 15, 1992

Roundtable

Edited by Ziva Freiman

On Attitudes to History

Frank Werner (moderator): We should use the time for direct discussion of the various opening statements, because the different opinions and positions have come out very clearly. Wolf, you had an objection to raise with Zaha?

Wolf Prix

Wolf Prix: Not really. But I've heard so many times that architecture is starting again, and I can't believe it. I think it is really the end. Maybe it will transform into other things, but architecture as we know it, as it is defined right now – this term that comes out of the nineteenth century – is dead. It's good this term is dead, because now we can redefine it. I think this [conference] could be a start, but we should throw away all the nineteenth-century stuff immediately: that means the "additive" way of thinking, that means [the obsession with] "defining" things, that means thinking in columns and beams. Therefore I appreciate the manifesto of Leb very much, because it's a kind of war.

If we look closely at what is happening in architecture now, I have to confess I'm really pessimistic, because what we [get to] do are very, very small projects, private projects. We are not concerned with schools; we are not concerned with public buildings; we are not concerned with universities; we are not concerned with hospitals; we are not concerned with social buildings – we are concerned with little, small bits and pieces, which are very philosophical, very theoretical, very good – spacey and spicy! But this is a very small sector, while tons of buildings are built by "holocaustian" people – by politicians and architects who have no attitude, no faith, no silence, no nothing. They are supported by a certain kind of paid press that makes us believe that this is architecture – and I think that that is the end.

Eric Moss: What is "the nineteenth century?" A swear word. It's a pejorative. Therefore [you suggest] getting rid of it all. But when one thinks about what you're saying, it has to do with the fact that you define yourself in opposition to something else that preceded you. Maybe your father, let's say. And to deny your father doesn't mean there's no father. It just means you're denying it. So there may be another level of this discussion,

which says that there's a use for a column or a beam, that it still has meaning, and in fact when you use one, you're using one in terms of the nineteenth-century discussion, and acting against it. Therefore you haven't gotten rid of that discussion at all.
Lebbeus Woods: No, I don't agree. It sounds like a monumental rationalization. Just taking the words from your statement, [Eric], when you said that all problems are the same problems – that's exactly the kind of rationalization every reactionary presents: to say, "Oh, there's nothing really new, we're not really in a new condition, it's just the same old thing, so let's just use the same old formulas."
Thom Mayne: That's not what is being said ...
Lebbeus Woods: I know [Eric] is not saying that, but it has the feel of that.
Eric Moss: It actually has to do with [Leb's] point about going to war. It's that everybody has to go to war, within the limits of the period at a certain time, and to leave the scene at a certain time. Now how has that condition changed? The guy [who made the drawings] in the cave at Altamira and the guy sitting in Vienna today face a very fundamental condition: of living and no longer living, and looking back and seeing it, and looking forward and seeing it.
Lebbeus Woods: Yes, but are there any conditions here in Vienna that weren't at Altamira?
Eric Moss: Almost all of them, and they're all secondary.
Lebbeus Woods: I don't think they're so secondary, because they are the substance of our life.
Eric Moss: That is a difficult fact. So far, the best metaphor [to illustrate the condition of contemporary architecture] is of fishing in a bathtub where there are no fish.
Lebbeus Woods: That's a nice metaphor, but I don't think it's the best so far ...
Eric Moss: For what?
Lebbeus Woods: You tell me. You're the one who said it was the best ...
Eric Moss: You said it was nice. Why is it nice?
Lebbeus Woods: It has a nice visual evocation to it, but why is it the best metaphor so far?
Eric Moss: Because, in the oddest way, it gives the pain of looking and not finding, of continuing to work and not necessarily getting there.
Lebbeus Woods: Maybe the reason I would say the fishing-in-the-bathtub metaphor is the best is because there's no chance of catching anything in the bathtub.
Steven Holl: Right. I want to pick up on that, because [in my opening statement] I brought up the bathtub metaphor as a provocation, as a question.

For me there is a symmetry in Lebbeus's statement, "I am an architect," with his passion in that declaration. I think architecture [as a profession] is in a different state: Leb has had more influence as an ar-

Lebbeus Woods

chitect than people who've built millions of square feet. When his *A+U* was published, it arrived in my hometown of Seattle, which I consider a completely backward city – almost no architecture has ever been built there – but in a way [Leb's published work] had more influence than a lot of buildings.

I think [architecture] is in a condition that is marginal. We work with one to two percent of buildings. When we have luck, maybe we build something. (Zaha has really been very lucky to get the Vitra Fire Station built.) This one to two percent is important. It's the culture of architecture. The rest of it is just building construction.

Eric Moss

Thom Mayne: I'd like to comment on Wolf's original statement. To me it's highly suspect. The method by which he defines the discussion is very simplistic, very dualistic: black and white, good and bad. It's an extremely simplified situation, where one can no longer look at history and see it the way we know it is – as evolutionary. And that, in fact, [history] allows us to prioritize, to place values.

I think the [current situation] requires extreme complexity in the method of investigation. It's not as simple as the situation that happened at the beginning of the century, which was perhaps necessary for breaking loose. [At this time], the agenda might be one of values, and establishing where we are vis-à-vis what is contemporary, what represents today versus what is a part of history that is still useful to us, which has value for us, and which represents a part of the positive social condition as a part of architecture.

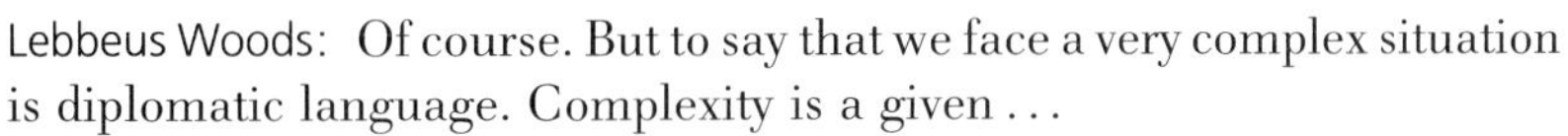

Lebbeus Woods: Of course. But to say that we face a very complex situation is diplomatic language. Complexity is a given ...

Thom Mayne: Not at all. I'm talking about the method of groundedness – the aspect of architecture which requires some connection. This is the discussion as I see it.

Eric Moss: [Leb], you weren't there yesterday [in London] in this discussion that came up, but I was saying to Danny Libeskind that we have to be careful not to assign all virtue to the [kind of] position [you have presented], and I think that is what is being said. You gave yourself sainthood in that. You attributed virtue to your position, and essentially denigrated every other position: "This is the way to do it! Do these things, and get rid of other things!" Somebody is actually telling you that there are other positions.

For example, what you said, and Wolf followed up, Sant'Elia already said: "Burn it every forty years." You're not the first guy to come along, and you're not going to be the last. In a sense that comes right out of the nineteenth century, which we're told we should get rid of.

Lebbeus Woods: That's the twentieth century.

Eric Moss: Just deal with the content of the discussion! We're not only suspicious of your position, you're suspicious of our position.

Lebbeus Woods: You're suspicious of everything, and you should be. I am, too. I cannot adopt a doctrine, therefore I have to create my own set of beliefs. I simply find it impossible to adopt a doctrine, and that includes a client's program that carries with it lots of doctrines that are assumed within the program.

Eric Moss: But that is a doctrine, it's a very clear doctrine.

Lebbeus Woods: What, program?

Eric Moss: You just deny [the typical client's approach of] "We'll have three conference rooms, two hospital beds, and a tree ..."

Lebbeus Woods: That's a doctrine.

Eric Moss: Okay, you're not adopting that. But you very clearly have a number of issues that you want to address. If one looks at your drawings, at the images, at how things are made, it is clear that you absolutely have a point of view. There are many things you include, and a hell of a lot you leave out. It's a very selective kind of doctrine.

Wolf Prix

Lebbeus Woods: Yes, but you said I was giving myself sainthood ...

Eric Moss: When you explain your work.

Lebbeus Woods: You said I had given myself sainthood, which means that I stand in some way above the common situation. Not at all. I find myself in the most common situation, which is that I can't adopt someone else's set of beliefs without questioning. I have to try, and I do fail. I could rip myself to shreds on this point.

Eric Moss: This is not a new discussion. That somebody would walk around with a candle in the darkness ...

Lebbeus Woods: You're the one who said nothing's new.

Eric Moss: That's exactly what I'm saying. To try to define a point of view for oneself, using what ammunition you can find along the way, in your head, outside of you, that's fine, that's commendable, but it's not novel.

Lebbeus Woods: I'm not talking about novelty. Novelty is not the point. Not my point, anyway.

Wolf Prix: Eric, I can't understand what you're saying. Nothing is new, and I have to accept it? The father is still there, whether I accept it or not? Give me a clue ...

Eric Moss: Leb said that [to claim that] the conditions are the same now as they were at Altamira is a rhetorical statement. Obviously the conditions are not the same; I'm saying that there are certain fundamental conditions of living, as I understand it, that have to be explained or dealt with, otherwise you can't take a step. You have to make some kind of map, you have to have some kind of strategy ...

Wolf Prix: What are those fundamental conditions?

Eric Moss: I was talking about the human limits.

Wolf Prix: What?

Eric Moss: You die.

Wolf Prix: Okay.

Eric Moss: Well, that's not so easy.

Wolf Prix: Eric, Eric, you were complaining we were playing Freud. You are Freud right now. It sounds very fundamentalistic, right for the explanation of the Ayatollah's architecture.

Eric Moss

Eric Moss: Yeah, but it might explain the cave paintings at Altamira, it might explain the guy sitting in the bathtub, fishing when there are no fish.
Wolf Prix: But, Eric, we have to solve some problems that are completely new, that never existed before. So why should we use tools out of the Stone Age to solve these problems?
Eric Moss: That's not what I said. The problem is always the same, but it comes out in different forms. The solutions are always different, because the problem always comes out in a different language. I'm saying two things. You're only hearing the first half. It's always different but it's always the same. The ways of dealing with it always change.
Wolf Prix: But this is simplifying a complex situation. That means one plus one is two, forever. We all die ... I don't get it.
Eric Moss: Well, why don't we turn it around, and why don't you tell us the novelties of the twenty-first century that haven't been dealt with, that we have to deal with.
Thom Mayne: New questions are replacing old questions, having to do with relevances of where we are and who we are. The problems don't have prescriptive answers regarding old things and new things. Maybe things like habitation in certain situations are related to the way things were done many, many years ago, prehistorically. Scratching and digging, right?

Thom Mayne

Wolf Prix: Yes, but we're not interested anymore in scratching and digging! That's done. I have the feeling this is a kind of insecurity, because we always have to go back to the roots.
Thom Mayne: Not at all. One of the issues is assessing the differences in the human species today and yesterday, and whether new institutions and new methodologies are required to resolve those. Some are and some aren't.
Wolf Prix: Thom, do you think we can solve the problem of a city of forty million by scratching and digging?
Thom Mayne: Of course not, it would be absurd. But it doesn't mean that there's nothing we can learn from it.
Eric Moss: There are still people with two arms and two legs living in that city, therefore there must be something that has to do with their history. Courage isn't only one-directional. Why is only one direction courageous?
Wolf Prix: So we stay at the stasis that one plus one is still two, because we are moving on two legs and writing with two hands. But maybe we should write with our eyes.

Defining a Public Agenda: The Public Interest, Architects and Power

Zaha Hadid

Zaha Hadid: The only way we can assess the [current] situation is by trying to diagnose the problems that have occurred. I think there is a great conflict between the interests of the architect, the interests of the public, and the interests of politics. I think the only way we can go forward is if these interests coincide in some way. That may take a long time. If we are seen as the evil force that destroys the city centers and the cities, we cannot push ahead.

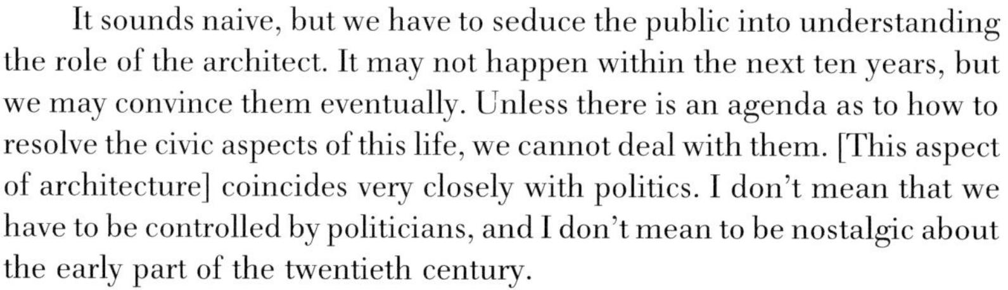

It sounds naive, but we have to seduce the public into understanding the role of the architect. It may not happen within the next ten years, but we may convince them eventually. Unless there is an agenda as to how to resolve the civic aspects of this life, we cannot deal with them. [This aspect of architecture] coincides very closely with politics. I don't mean that we have to be controlled by politicians, and I don't mean to be nostalgic about the early part of the twentieth century.

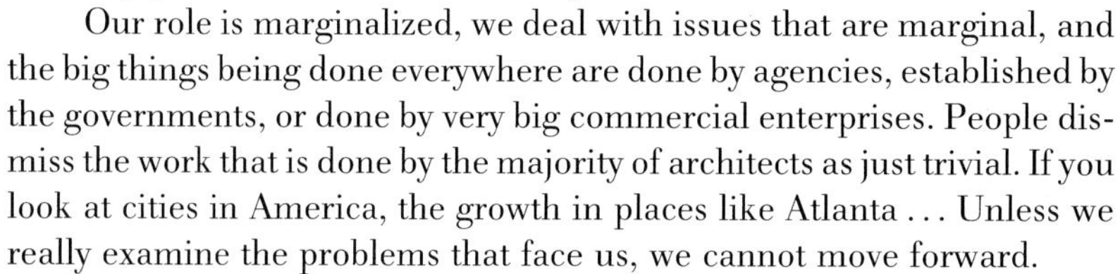

Our role is marginalized, we deal with issues that are marginal, and the big things being done everywhere are done by agencies, established by the governments, or done by very big commercial enterprises. People dismiss the work that is done by the majority of architects as just trivial. If you look at cities in America, the growth in places like Atlanta ... Unless we really examine the problems that face us, we cannot move forward.

Lebbeus Woods: Part of the problem is, who defines the public interest?

Zaha Hadid: I don't think it's definable in an hour. It has to be a collective interest.

Lebbeus Woods: Who is the collective? – that's what I'm getting at. We speak for architects, but, let's face it, we wouldn't want most architects to have real autonomy, because they're not producing good architecture, they're not capable of it. When we say architects, we're being very liberal in our inclusion, but we're talking about a few architects.

Zaha Hadid: I'm talking more about the next generation of architects. That's why I think the role of the teacher at this time is very important. I'm only referring to the condition in London, where I have observed very carefully what is happening in the schools, and which I find extremely worrying.

For the first time in many years, I've reacted very violently; I have to reconsider my position as a teacher because of this avoidance of architecture [in the schools], and [the lack of] understanding regarding the role of conceptual art and its impact on architecture. Not understanding the degree of self-indulgence imposed by teachers on students creates a void in this culture! I remember when I was a student in the seventies, this void created a gap in the understanding of what we can do to move forward. Therefore the only thing you can do is to resort to historical models. It *is* fundamentalist. It is exactly what happened with the Ayatollah, it was because there was a lack of belief in any role of the future.

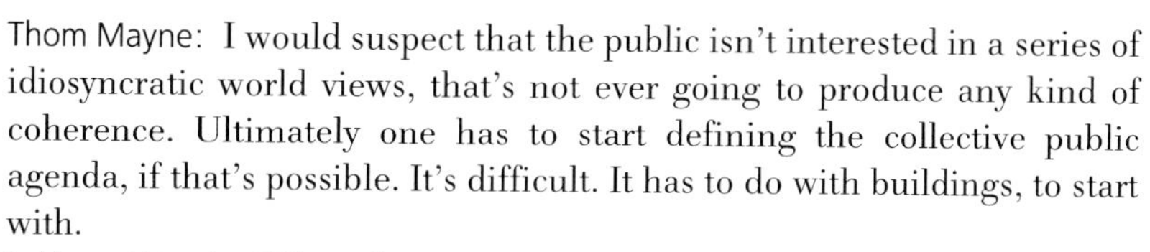

Thom Mayne: I would suspect that the public isn't interested in a series of idiosyncratic world views, that's not ever going to produce any kind of coherence. Ultimately one has to start defining the collective public agenda, if that's possible. It's difficult. It has to do with buildings, to start with.

Lebbeus Woods

Lebbeus Woods: Who does that? Who defines the collective public agenda?

Thom Mayne: The architectural community. It has to.

Lebbeus Woods: Who?

Thom Mayne: Us.

Lebbeus Woods: Us?

Thom Mayne: Absolutely. Unless you want to give the power out. Only by bridging the gap can you establish an agenda …

Lebbeus Woods: But here you have the dilemma …

Zaha Hadid: I think it's in many layers of society. I don't think it can be done only by architects. It has to be done by writers, philosophers, moviemakers, people who observe the way people live, and respond to it.

Lebbeus Woods: You don't want George Bush defining the public interest. In Croatia now, the politicians there have an opportunity to rebuild a society, but again it's the same old swamp. They're defining the public interest in the most reactionary way.

Zaha Hadid: The politicians' interest is definitely revisionary. It's a revisionist tendency, and this occurs everywhere.

Lebbeus Woods: Exactly.

Zaha Hadid: That's the reason I think in time the only way one should operate is to overlap [with other disciplines], because [society] is very diverse.

Eric Moss: There's another way to look at it. Wolf was talking about this work we do as on the edge, as marginal – in other words, what we do is really the small stuff. There's a very old Chinese philosopher, Sun Tzu, who wrote a book called *The Art of War*. It teaches you how to attack … It's actually very subtle, not [like the strategies taught at] Sandhurst or West Point, but how to find where the [opponents] are vulnerable, and go there.

Eric Moss

To hope for enlightened political and economic establishments on Wall Street, or Downing Street, or the White House, is really naive. For me, the way to do it is to push the people you know, who are your friends, whether it's the people here at this table, or someone else. You get into the cracks, just like Sun Tzu said, and you push out that way. You go where it's vulnerable. You go where they're weak.

Wolf Prix: Eric, this is so naive. This is so naive, I can't believe it!

Eric Moss: Well, what is not naive?

Wolf Prix: This is so naive, believing that architects can get power. If we were interested in power, we would be politicians. I heard it in '68, Hollein was talking the same way. In '68, people said, "We have to go through the institutions. We'll get the power. We will change it …"

Eric Moss: I said you go around it. The power is not homogeneous. It's not everywhere. You go where you can go and you build out from that.
Wolf Prix: Eric, strategy, Machiavelli, and all this stuff, we had it. It's done. It doesn't work.
Eric Moss: What works?
Wolf Prix: The "two percent" [influential minority] may work. The media may work. The fact that [Lebbeus Woods] is more influential than Skidmore Owings & Merrill may work ...
Eric Moss: That's the crack! That's exactly what it is ...

Carme Pinós

Clients and Competitions

Wolf Prix: You can see it on the tables of the students, that now Leb is the star. He's very influential. But on the other hand, I heard it several times from young people that there's no work, they can't get through because "you guys don't build." We are losing one competition after another against normal, so-called "obedient" projects. ... The [unfavorable client's] argument is: "[Your building is] 15 percent more expensive! You want [me] to build it?" So you can say, okay, knowing that, I'll never slant a beam again, because I know I will lose the project. This is the problem of our profession.
Eric Moss: Just hypothetically you could say "Okay, find the guy who has 15 percent more money ..."
Wolf Prix: Yes, but this is like praying for rain in the desert. We can be magicians ... I can do the rain-dance with you.
Frank Werner: If we reduce the problem this way, we can finish the conference by saying that the clients are the real deconstructivists – not you, but the clients – they are destroying everything ...

[Carme Pinós's Igualada] cemetery is in a very traditional farmhouse region. I visited it with my students. It is incredible how, in such a provincial, remote little village, the mayor could build such a cemetery. In Germany, this would be absolutely impossible, for all the reasons you have mentioned. But nevertheless, it was realized!
Eric Moss: It seems to me that you take something on, and you expect to get resistance. A riot!
Carme Pinós: In our country we have a lot of difficulties with our work; we won the competition for the cemetery because the jury was [made up of] architects and they understood our proposition. But the discussion with the mayor is an interpretation of the program. We spoke all the time about his kind of program, [about statistics like] the number of dead ... We held meetings with the people of the village, we spoke and worked in their language. We worked with the traditional culture, with the culture of everyday life, we just interpreted it in a different way. Now they see the result.
Frank Werner: Let me ask you another question. Do you feel that you have educated the client?

Carme Pinós: Yes.
Eric Moss: She lied to the client, that's what she did!
Carme Pinós: No, this is the thing I want to say: always to interpret the program, to interpret the place, and to play with them.

For example, recently I participated in a competition in Mont-Saint-Michel to resolve the awful problems that exist there now. The reality of that place is a disaster. They want to get rid of the cars, to get rid of the tourists; but I tried to turn their concept upside down. The tourists are not awful, the tourists are fantastic; the cars can be fine ... it's a reality. A historical monument exists partly because the tourists exist. It's all an interpretation of the program ...

[Architects have] to be complicit with fate, to play, to make a dialogue. Our reality is as good as the reality of years ago, [although] now it is much more difficult. Because before, the architect was the servant of the power and the power was very clear – in religion, and the aristocracy. The bourgeoisie is much more complex, chaotic. Should architecture now be in the service of that?!
Wolf Prix: Did you win the competition? Is it decided?
Carme Pinós: No. [laughter]
Steven Holl: I think that this issue of competitions is very important. If we could get some consensus here on the idea that competitions should not be interfered with ...
Lebbeus Woods: How do you get such a consensus?
Steven Holl: [Competitions are] a way that architecture can actually occur. Some of us, like Bernard Tschumi, were lucky to squeak through the crack of allowing the competition-winning scheme to be built as it was designed. I think if we had built the [American Memorial] library in Berlin, we could have made a kind of radical architecture within the system that exists, but it was interfered with.[1] [See page 126 for the notes.]
Wolf Prix: But this is not by chance.
Steven Holl: This is the main issue, because [competitions are] a way of making architecture without an authoritarian government; it's a way of doing it democratically. The competitions, the [winning] schemes, must be respected and they must be built. This business about having a false competition [for the Ronacher Theater] in Vienna is a complete scam.[2]

Helmut Swiczinsky

Peter Noever: This is standard in Vienna. And in other countries it's quite similar.
Zaha Hadid: Not all competitions everywhere are a scam. One should not go into them only thinking that one must win them. Competitions are very useful tools of learning. It's the one time you can allow yourself to be innocent again. I think it's very important. Of course, it's very painful to win the competition and then see the project built by someone else.

Recently, I went to the factory in Germany, which is under the name of Stirling.[3] It wasn't done by Stirling, but by his office and by Walter Nageli. This is a competition that was won by someone else. The client decided he did not want the first prize, but the second prize ... and the

second prize was actually better than the first prize. So there are always ironies in these situations ... [but] I don't think the issue of entering competitions should be a negative one.
Steven Holl: No, in fact, in Finland, almost every public building is done by competition, and they are done quite correctly, but they are restricted to Finnish architects.
Zaha Hadid: In England there aren't enough competitions; at least in Germany, France, Switzerland, there are some, but England doesn't operate this way. The scene is operated within the particular brotherhood – Masonic temple – it is totally behind closed doors, it is dished out among a very small number of people ... there is no public [input].

Carme Pinós

Wolf Prix: But Steve, don't you believe that it is not by chance that your design was cancelled?
Steven Holl: I think it was chance. Because if Nagel had not been elected building senator – which was the political thing that occurred right in the middle of everything, when we had already won the competition – this building would have been built. We even had the unanimous approval of the librarians. They sent out the public referendum on the building and we won the vote but Nagel suppressed the information, and ran another mock competition and killed us.
Wolf Prix: It's the personal decision of a jerk.
Steven Holl: Yes. I also believe in the "fate things."
Lebbeus Woods: I think that this conversation is boiling down to who got to build what building.
Wolf Prix: No, Leb, this is just proof that there is a connection between obedient things and disobedient things, and the cancellation of disobedient things.

[In a recent presentation at the Cooper Union in New York], your developer, [Eric], a bright guy, tried for an hour to prove how he is on the right track; that he can make money out of your things, and so forth. I am just asking myself why isn't that an example for more developers when it is so easy to do, and if one can make so much money out of it? I tell you it's very frightening ... this is connected to the obedience of architects.

Steven Holl

Reprise: The Role of the Architect, or Power and Fulfillment

Frank Werner: I would like to come back to the question: what is the role of the architect today? Is he or she the agent of the mighties, is he a designer of a neutral space for neutral people? Does he have to be an agent provocateur? (I personally believe that all architects, all over the world, must always be agents provocateurs.) Or should we go back to the concept of architecture as weapon that we had fifty years ago?
Wolf Prix: Okay. I'll tell you what we think we are. We are Formula One race-car drivers without salary. We have our circuits, we are going very

very fast through curves, and we can't handle this balance between life and death in architecture. A lot of people, about two percent of the entire population, are looking at this circus, but we have really no influence in culture. The culture is like a herd of elephants trampling over our buildings; meanwhile, we are driving very fast and very dangerously ...

Thom Mayne: But Wolf, that's not going to change until we can define an agenda that makes any type of connection beyond personal desire ...

Wolf Prix: Maybe some of you teachers ...

Thom Mayne: And you have to articulate [a more broadly engaged] position because [otherwise] no one is going to care, and they shouldn't care! Because it's your private, personal world view! You've got eight people that agree with you.

Wolf Prix: But that is what I am saying. It's a private agenda. So we lost every ...

Peter Noever

Peter Noever: But the question is whether it is wrong to lose on this point, or is it right? What you, [Wolf], mentioned is a power game. It's a question of what architecture has to do with art. If you make art, you don't care if it's accepted or not, you just continue your work. This [can be] a problem with architecture that wants to be avant-garde, that wants to be art, [because] then you need this kind of power to realize [your work]. It's on this borderline, on this knife-edge ...

Eric Moss: With respect, there's a huge amount of self-pity in that race-car driver analogy, as romantic as it is; I think it has a lot of appeal if you think of yourself careening around in a Porsche, or [that] you're going to blow yourself up. And it's like that Brueghel painting, where Icarus falls and nobody gives a damn.

Lebbeus Woods: They make paintings about it.

Eric Moss: But the point is that Kafka had a hell of a tough time publishing anything, and so did Nietzsche. [You're saying], "It's so easy to paint! It's so easy to write! You know what's hard? The only hard thing on the planet is to be an architect." *Impossible!* It's not true.

Wolf Prix: But, my dear friend, we are not talking about writing, we are not talking about music. We are talking about architecture!

Eric Moss: Everyone who is creative is under the same kind of pressure.

Wolf Prix: Yes, I know, I know, but we are talking about architecture and not about writing. And not about music. Music is much harder! Because you have to be good to be on top. That thank God we don't have to do. Come on, Eric.

Eric Moss

Eric Moss: And I am saying that it's difficult if you have something you want to get out, and you want to get it out untouched, and you don't want to be obedient to somebody ...

Wolf Prix: Give me an example!

Eric Moss: An example of what?

Wolf Prix: Of what you are talking about!

Eric Moss: I'll give you a very good example, and one that you know, which has to do with getting certain written material published, and nobody wants to publish it! They won't publish it, period. "Who is your agent? How famous are you? Who are you? What's the subject? We don't know what the subject is! Is it religion, is it history? Come back when you are famous, we'll publish you." There is no difference! My consolation to you is that everybody who does what he wants to do has to fight through that problem. The fact of the matter is that [Coop Himmelblau's] rooftop [lawyer's office] got built somehow ...

Wolf Prix: That was a lucky punch!

Eric Moss: So what? A few lucky punches and you've got ...

Wolf Prix: Let me remind you that [as jurors last year, Steve Holl and I] were looking for schools, hospitals, and other things [among the submissions to] the *P/A* Awards. And we couldn't find anything like that for the award, because it was shit stuff. So this is what I'm talking about, nothing else. I am not mourning that we don't get more commissions, that is the wrong way of understanding what I said ... We have to face the fact that we are on the edge. I don't say it is bad, or it is good, I just say we are on the edge and we have no influence.

Eric Moss: And therefore what?

Wolf Prix: Therefore we have to reconsider what we are doing.

Eric Moss: And what conclusion did you come to?

Wolf Prix: My proposal would be the end of architecture.

Eric Moss: To quit.

Wolf Prix: Yeah, we will quit. After this conference we quit. [laughter]

Wolf Prix

Reprise: The Public Dimension of Architecture versus the Exotic Project

Lebbeus Woods: To use the phrase that Peter Noever invented, we are all able to function on some level as "exotic project-makers" – in other words, artists, people who can squeak out by random luck an exotic project that gets a lot of publicity. Everyone says this person is a great architect-artist and yet, the world goes on pretty much without any reference to this particular kind of exotic project.

So, I want to put to myself a question in front of this group, because I am really curious: is your ambition for architecture anything other than to make exotic projects? Or is there a desire to make present the public, or universal, dimension inherent in the idea of architecture? And then how do you reconcile that with the exotic project that by random luck you manage to get through? I think this is the important question – otherwise, it's just about a series of lucky shots.

Wolf Prix: We are the field of lucky shots, yes, we have to admit that.

Steven Holl: I don't think so ...

Lebbeus Woods: What is the public dimension of your project?

Steven Holl: This is where Lebbeus and I disagree. I believe in actually engaging the program, really getting your hands on the program, and

Thom Mayne

doing something with it – such as in the Berlin library the idea of a browsing circuit, which was to open up the whole library to whoever passes through it, or [in the Palazzo del Cinema project] in Venice, the idea of a huge public grotto, which was to give back [a public place] to the Lido community[4] – this idea of the program for me is very important.

Wolf Prix: Now I know why you lost the [library] project. I'm sure! At the very end [the Berlin official] could argue that opening up the library is more dangerous because blah blah blah blah.

Steven Holl

Steven Holl: That is the pessimistic view. I'm answering [Leb's] question about the exotic, one-off thing. I think that in fact each project has a locus of relations. We [built] a housing project in [Fukuoka], Japan, where there were no walls, all the walls are [pivoting]; bedrooms could be added or subtracted. That has some relationship to the problem of housing. You don't have to build a thousand housing units to have an effect on what the possible next dimension in making urban housing would be, in some relation to the city.

Wolf Prix: This is true.

Lebbeus Woods: But wait a minute! A lot of reference in our work and in our discourse does relate back to the early part of the century, let's face it, all of us. But if you really look at what went on there, it wasn't about accepting the fabric of relationships that existed. Everything that was promised by modern architecture was [predicated on] a new set of relationships. That was the whole premise of all of this work that has reverberated down through this century, this epoch. It was based on the promise of new relationships between people, a new fabric of society. Where is that today? Where is that in this discourse? I don't hear it. I hear people trying to accommodate themselves to what is, in order to make the exotic projects.

Carme Pinós

Thom Mayne: If I were to broaden this and put it into political terms, I would say that in the first part of the century there was a paradigm that advanced notions of unification, which were totally connected to a very idealistic, progressive idea of social, democratic institutions. That was a global paradigm. In the second half of the century there is a very different set of ideas that questions the other side of unification – which has to do with a suppression of difference. And in fact, we are now looking at a discussion of the same social democratic institutions, except they are no longer prioritizing majorities, but minorities.

Los Angeles happens to be one of the cities [where this is happening]. There is no way of talking [about L. A.] in terms of majorities; it's a city that is made only of minorities. Now that allows for another discussion that, in fact, preferences the idiosyncratic – the reverse of unification, which [Leb] is talking about.

We should keep in mind that [our position] is a minority position, it is not a majority position – and it's an important discussion because it puts [our situation] within a larger perspective.

Lebbeus Woods: Yes, but what kind of minority are you talking about here?

Thom Mayne: I am talking about any number of them, economic, or ethnic, or whatever ... Los Angeles speaks some 120 languages ...
Lebbeus Woods: But, let me just follow up. Is this then the question of the exotic project, to use this term? How does [the emphasis on minority] not simply co-opt [the architecture] into the latest fashion of the time?
Thom Mayne: I don't understand what you are talking about. "Exotic project" means nothing to me.
Lebbeus Woods: Okay. It is the product that exists only once ...
Steven Holl: ... like a human being ...
Lebbeus Woods: ... in a sea of non-architecture ...
Thom Mayne: So the analogue would be our own personalities as exotic?
Lebbeus Woods: Yes, exactly.
Steven Holl: This exotic work could be the reassertion of individuality. I went yesterday to visit the 1932 Werkbund, and I was shocked, because in Stuttgart at least there was a little bit of difference, but here, in the Vienna Werkbund, everyone just falls into line. The white vocabulary is completely adhered to. In a way they believed altogether in this ideological frame.

Today, it has totally shifted; the assertion of the individual is a very important thing. It's the one thing in housing that I think you could contribute, on a marginal scale: the insertion of individual space, of the idiosyncractic. You call it exotic, but I think there is a positive dimension to it.

Zaha Hadid

Zaha Hadid: I think what differentiates this century from the nineteenth is that in the twentieth century there was an accommodation of mass culture. The masses became the client, fundamentally, and therefore one tried to invent ideas to accommodate the masses – whether those were civic centers, civic spaces, housing for the populace ...

I think that the two worlds – of the singular client and of the masses – could [co]exist. If you go to Berlin, you can see utopian housing projects of the 1920s and the 1930s, like the Gross-Siedlung Britz, and you can still see two beautiful houses by Luckhardt and Anker. They both occurred in the same period, they are still very good.

But we really have to look at how to accommodate for the masses in a successful way, because this is fundamentally who our client should be. If we look at the future – how are we going to live in the twenty-first century, what is the idea of work in the twenty-first century? If we operate on the idea of fewer work days, what are people going to do in the rest of their time? How do we then invent spaces to accommodate for this shift in culture?

This shift in culture is inevitable; in England it is phenomenal. When I came to England fifteen years ago, there were hardly any Indians, very few blacks, and this has changed totally. And the use of the city has changed. In London fifteen years ago all the English went out to the countryside, to their country homes on the weekend, the city was empty.

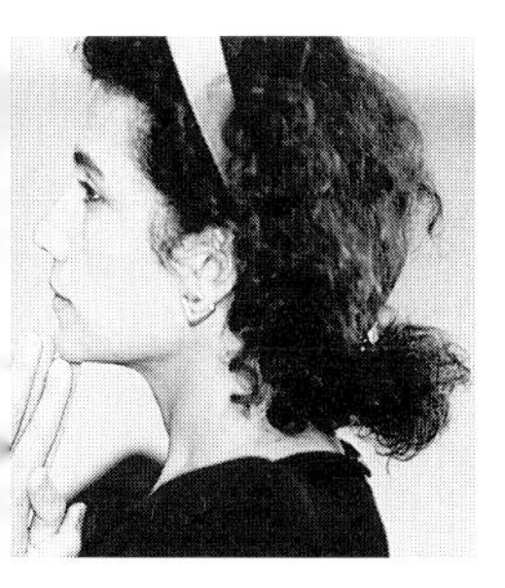

Carme Pinós

London on Sundays now is more crowded than on a weekday, because of the minorities who all live outside, and are coming in to see the city.
Thom Mayne: Reminds me of Los Angeles, the second-largest city in Mexico!
Zaha Hadid: I know it will take a long time, but this is what we have to address. I know that the picture is very bleak ...
Eric Moss: In fact it is very discouraging if you talk about it in those terms ...
Lebbeus Woods: I am glad to hear Zaha talk like this!
Eric Moss: Looking at the situation [after the riots] in Los Angeles, when you drive around a little bit, you see blocks that are untouched; then all of a sudden you come to the line of Korean businesses, and they are burned to the ground. [Such] animosity between groups of people – it's an adversarial city in many ways.

Many of the big cities in America, and now in Europe as well, have those kinds of problems – they are contentious as hell! It's like a balkanization of the cities. And when you were talking before about how to find a way to live in the twenty-first century, you are still talking [only] about what the white middle class is going to do ...
Zaha Hadid: I don't think so!
Eric Moss: I don't think anybody is working on how those people [in the inner cities] are going to live in the twenty-first century ...
Zaha Hadid: I think we have to shut our egos and maybe form an agency that deals with housing. I look at London again, at the Architectural Association. They have these programs at school that deal with housing, energy ... and they do it in the most banal, awful way. They do housing in the Third World – there is no reason for the West to be patronizing towards the Third World! They can still do interesting housing. The experiment in housing is not yet over. I say, take these very basic programs and look at them. I don't say we have to build them right away, but look at them.
Eric Moss: I could be extremely sympathetic to that from the point of view of an individual architect making an imprint with a housing project, including a rotating wall, let's say, that would have an impact, would move the discussion on housing. But it occurs on a relatively tiny scale, among relatively few architects.

In American cities, the scale of the problem [we] are talking about requires the kind of interests that don't seem to be forthcoming – political interest, and economic interest, and a priority on these [troubled] places. If you listen to the people talking about this L. A. conflagration, everybody is lying! It didn't happen, or it happened because the morals are weak – nobody is even dealing with the substance of the problem. So it would be reasonable in a societal sense, or in an urban sense, to be extremely pessimistic about these cities in the United States. That doesn't exclude the possibility of interesting things taking place on the way down, which are signs of optimism in the dark.

Zaha Hadid

Zaha Hadid: That's neither here nor there. One has to address a variety of issues. Okay, the situation now is bad, but I don't think one should assume it will always be like this. We have to find a way of changing it, and we might not succeed, but I'm saying through education in twenty years' time we might achieve something. It is not so immediate.
Eric Moss: My sense is that you tend to go to the problems or to the point where you can make something. That may be what everyone has in common here, in spite of everything else: a level of intention to work in a certain way.
Zaha Hadid: You can deal with [personal architectural preoccupations and broader societal issues] simultaneously!
Eric Moss: I wouldn't mind believing that, if you could cite some indication that it is possible.
Zaha Hadid: I think it is possible.
Peter Noever: What Zaha mentioned is concerned more with a new definition of architecture. Maybe the projects, as I listen to this discussion, are as radical as all of you probably believe. We speak about what is very romantic, and what we could look for ... but on the other hand, maybe nobody is getting the message of this architecture.

Peter Noever

There is nothing in this architecture that is elitist. All the projects you are doing are "housing projects," all of it is for a mass culture. In this respect the work is not exotic, except in the sense of being unique, and very small in scale. The problem is, if the compromises you make are too big, because you have become frustrated after a while and it seems that everybody is making more compromises, then [you risk] killing your own work. Every one of you is well known, is quite a star, all the magazines are full [of your work], but nobody is reaching [the audience]. Maybe it's the problem of the media, of publication.
Thom Mayne: Maybe that is what we all share, though.
Wolf Prix: But Peter, isn't that the question of a certain type of climate that allows the architects to push the envelope with their projects? Sometimes you can do it, and sometimes it is impossible.

I still think that now we have a big swing to the right, a reactionary political scene that makes it impossible to experiment with architecture. If you open up systems in architecture that allow an open library, the political system says no. I don't know how we can fight that, except by emigrating.
Peter Noever: But where? Where would you go?
Thom Mayne: Wolf, aren't you premising the whole discussion on the realization of built work? It's not always possible to realize [every idea].

I wouldn't have assessed the problem in L. A. the way you did, Eric, at all. I would have said there are a lot of people discussing the problem, it's quite clear! There is an enormous discrepancy between rich and poor, the largest since the twenties: one percent of the population in the United States now has wealth [equivalent to that] of the bottom 90 percent. It's a racist culture and we still haven't confronted the racism. It's an open

Thom Mayne

discussion: it doesn't have to be particularly architectural – it's a political discussion. But one would have to participate in that to be able to talk about architecture's role.

Wolf Prix: Thom, are you talking about *literature*?!

Thom Mayne: Of course not.

Wolf Prix: I'm talking about moving the body through the built space.

Thom Mayne: Look at the group here. You contribute in all kinds of ways, it's not simply just realizing construction.

Wolf Prix: But, Thom, if we escape to a kind of tower of publications, or just drawings which are not allowed to be built ...

Thom Mayne: But the issue isn't publication. The issue is your own work, and if you are contributing to these problems, or coming up with new alternatives ...

Wolf Prix: You think so?

Thom Mayne: I am not talking about publication, that's secondary ...

Peter Noever: So what you are talking about is status quo. That nothing is possible or it is very difficult. But this is not the way out. Everyone who is sitting here knows that.

Eric Moss: Actually, what is being said is quite interesting. Because Wolf is saying if you don't build it, you've failed. And Thom is saying if you can't build it, aside from going out and voting, you can talk about it, write about it, draw it – at which point somebody else may pick it up and build it.

Wolf Prix: One thing: if you can explain a movie, it's not worth doing the movie. If you can explain architecture, it's not worth building it. I still think that the built architecture adds a certain level to the society ...

Thom Mayne: Of course it does.

Eric Moss: Nobody would argue against that.

Lebbeus Woods: I might argue against it but I'm not going to do that right now.

Zaha Hadid: For me, built or unbuilt, one is not more important than the other. I think one learns a great deal by doing projects, and they have a purpose.

Wolf Prix: Zaha, if it is built, it is not better or worse, this is not the question. But I think it adds a new experience ...

Zaha Hadid: Oh, definitely it does.

Wolf Prix: So this is what I am talking about.

Zaha Hadid: Wolf, I understand your anger and I sympathize with it

Wolf Prix: This is not an anger ...

Zaha Hadid: ... I do. Because many times I am angry about very similar things. But we cannot afford to waste our energy at this kind of anger. We have to re-direct it.

Wolf Prix: Zaha, don't confuse my aggressive language with anger that I lost a project ...

Zaha Hadid: I'm not thinking about that at all. You are luckier than me, because I live in England, which is a very strange condition ... [laughter] ... much worse than Austria by any means. And that is why I sympathize

with your anger. I just think that one has to somehow find ways to move forward in a positive way.
Wolf Prix: I agree.
Zaha Hadid: I don't have the recipe for it, I just think that it's something that is going to take time ... I think that it also has to do with the [need for] conversation between people of different professions, different generations ...
Wolf Prix: But even democracy has weapons to kill ideas by censorship – in a very unconscious way. It is not by chance that he and he and he cannot build! [There] is the secret censorship that is called taste; the [overt] argument is, "We don't like these guys because they can't build, it's too complicated, it's leaking ..."
Thom Mayne: But, Wolf, that has been happening for two thousand years. There's always a complacency to the normative ... it has always existed.
Lebbeus Woods: I know your work, [Thom], and I know that there is a complexity in your work. But maybe the habit of dealing with clients, which I haven't had to do, has formed this kind of language, this kind of delicate tight-rope act between, shall we say, assuaging the clients, and yet asserting your own point of view, as it has developed?

You've mentioned CIAM and Team X. I wonder what would happen if out of this group some kind of public statement could come – and I know it won't, because we haven't prepared [for it]. But if a kind of polemic, a kind of assertion about architecture can come [out of this meeting], rather than each of us going back and trying to snake our way through this process, that would be a much more radical position. But I have the feeling that each one of us is isolated, alone, fighting our own little battle, trying to get through by tricks – by lying, as Eric called it. That deprives the whole thing of a kind of collective.

Zaha, I loved hearing what you said and I think you are absolutely right. My own instinct is to find a way to join our individuality with other human beings; I don't know how many, I can't say masses, but I can say other human beings. Unless we proclaim some idea, it all ends up as a very isolated event.
Thom Mayne: The next question is whether that is even possible.
Lebbeus Woods: Well, that's open for debate, but I think it is possible. The idea that each individual is finding some way to work in the world is in fact the basis for a community of individuals.
Zaha Hadid: Again, I think that you can maintain your identity as an individual and be a part of a collective. One has to operate naturally – you have to be able to maintain this identity and also work within a community.
Lebbeus Woods: Of course, but what is the community you are speaking of?
Zaha Hadid: I am not talking about a collective workshop of architects. And you will not have a manifesto in a day. This might result in a series of meetings.

Lebbeus Woods

Lebbeus Woods: I hope it does result in a series of meetings.
Thom Mayne: It might be the only hope to de-marginalize [architecture].
Lebbeus Woods: Because this group of people right here doesn't have power, but we have a certain authority. Magazines will print what we do, people will report what we say. Wolf may not agree with this, but we do have a certain authority, and it's just a matter of asserting it, and not simply compromising the authority of our voices in order to slide into the next possible slot, in a kind of expedient move ...
Wolf Prix: But explain to me, authority over whom? Students?
Lebbeus Woods: No, no, no. Authority over ideas.

Reprise: New Clients, New Programs

Peter Noever: Eric has the client he needs, but for others it might be a problem. I think that the question could be how to create the right clients. This is one of the problems of this society – because democracy or not, there are no clients! The client is the media, maybe, because they like everything that is colorful, everything that is a little bit different, they use it; you are very much used by the media at the same time. But the question, and Zaha also mentioned it, is how to create a new client.

This has much to do with the understanding of the culture. The art market, for example, is a kind of client, [though it is] broken down at the moment. Somebody making installations – which is close to a kind of [experimental] architecture and very expensive – couldn't survive if there wasn't an art market. It's a very similar problem, because if the artists are too close to the art market, maybe they lose the power of their own art. So, the point is how to make an atmosphere [conducive] to the creation of a new client?

I believe also in Wolf's position that it's important [to build]. One can make it in theory, one can make drawings, [but] the sensation of space in three dimensions has a different point to it.
Thom Mayne: Don't you need an agenda first? You work on the idea and then decide whether it is worth disseminating. It seems that we need the agenda first; the client is a second issue.

Peter Noever: Yes, sure ... but it's very strange that there is one guy, Rolf Fehlbaum at Vitra, who is inviting people to do work like Zaha's fire station or Gehry's museum. This is exotic, very unique. ... but there is no atmosphere to [support] what is done here [in Vienna, although] there is a lot that is done.
Frank Werner: But you have to create the atmosphere.
Peter Noever: That is the question, how? How?
Frank Werner: When the [Ronacher] Theater project by Coop Himmelblau was cancelled, I had a phone conversation with the Lord Mayor of Vienna and it was such an absurd discussion because I tried to talk with him in architectonic terms and he in political terms. He was completely unable to understand any architectonic argument, [he showed] no interest at all.
Eric Moss: Why did he call you?
Frank Werner: To protest.
Eric Moss: So you called him.
Frank Werner: No, he called me. I had written a letter and he feared that I would publish it.
Thom Mayne: [You have to] shift the discussion. This is what we were talking about earlier: "This is how you get into the building, and this is how you get out of it." So, make it a political discussion, make it a discussion that relates to the enterprise.
Lebbeus Woods: You see, that's a problem. If you try to sell your idea in terms of your client's agenda you're always going to lose. There are exceptions, but ninety-nine times out of a hundred you're going to lose. You can't sell it on the grounds that good design is more economical. It isn't more economical! It's got to have another basis. It isn't just a matter of the efficacy of entry and exit, Thom. You can't say it works better. Maybe it doesn't work better!

Steven Holl

If it really is a critical piece of work, it might be like Richard Serra's sculpture in the Federal Building Plaza in New York, which interrupted the flow of pedestrians moving across that space – and it was torn down, by the way, because of that simple fact! It offended the idea of efficacy. So, as soon as you start arguing in terms of your client's agenda, I think you are lost. We have to set our own agenda.
Zaha Hadid: I would say that there is a degree of generosity among us. We may be critical of each other's work, but at the same time be generous with a degree of camaraderie. I think [some mutal support] is possible.
Eric Moss: I think that [fellow feeling] happens, and it happens in awfully strong ways. I actually feel carried along by it, because otherwise it's completely hopeless. For me that is maybe the most important thing about something like this [conference]. You don't quite know whether that's a consolation, or that's all there is, but it's helpful.

If you looked around and asked where clients are coming from – the new clients Peter was talking about – one of the things that you wind up asking for is a kind of statism. [Peter] said maybe the state will produce them. Someone then asked: "Which state?" and that was not a bad question.

Zaha Hadid: The welfare state. [laughter]

Eric Moss: Well, yeah, but the welfare state is in the tank! The welfare state isn't doing it. The welfare state can't make its schools, can't build its hospitals! Then you look to the universities, let's say, universities in America, for instance, which are supposed to be the source of ideas, and which don't have to amortize their buildings over twenty-five years ... So you look at the universities, and what do you see? Not a hell of a lot! What you come down to is private assignment of work. For us that may be the most [we can expect].

[Like Zaha's] client for the fire station, there are some of those people around who have enough largesse, and enough interest, and who are supportive enough, and I think that's where the action comes from now. They can be encouraged. I don't see where else it's going to come from. Or what about the President of France, who is supposed to be a cultured guy?!

Lebbeus Woods: What about [it coming] from the architects? What do the architects have to contribute, other than the skill of design?

Thom Mayne: When there is a void in the issues, doesn't it depend on an intelligent body stepping in? Over lunch we were discussing the shift in education over the last fifty to a hundred years having to do with [the "segregation" of the] liberal arts: a doctor, for instance, is no longer really able to participate at a useful level in society, to resolve issues of ethics – which may be the most important human issues today in medicine! Yet, doctors are not qualified because they choose not to be qualified, or there is no one to step forward to fulfill that goal and it's left to somebody else.

[Or, an opposite example is] the way artists function in theology or philosophy, asking certain types of questions [at this point] in the twentieth century [that are not being addressed by] the traditional theological institutions. I think it's a matter of stepping forward; if you have something to say, you fill the gap. You participate in the process.

Eric Moss

Lebbeus Woods: That is exactly why I am asking the question – what are we saying about our work?

Steven Holl: I think that's something we haven't really touched on; we are going around this political issue. If we were to try to come to some kind of agreement, I think one point would be that we should build a new architecture; we are of this generation, we are of this time, and there is a necessity to build it. I don't think that anyone here is arguing for a historical position.

Another point, linked to that, [is the need for] new programs. We had some agreement about the possibility of "hybrid programs," which would mean different kinds of institutions, which would redefine what the institution of the library, for instance, [could be] when hybridized with x, y, and z; what kind of space in the city, in the metropolis, we would come up with in proposing an airport hybridized with x, y, and z.

I strongly believe that we must engulf the program – [the experiment with programs yields] new experiences in space: to actually move the body through space in a very dynamic way, which has never been done. I can't wait to walk through this fire station. I think these poor firemen, their boots might fall off ... [laughter]

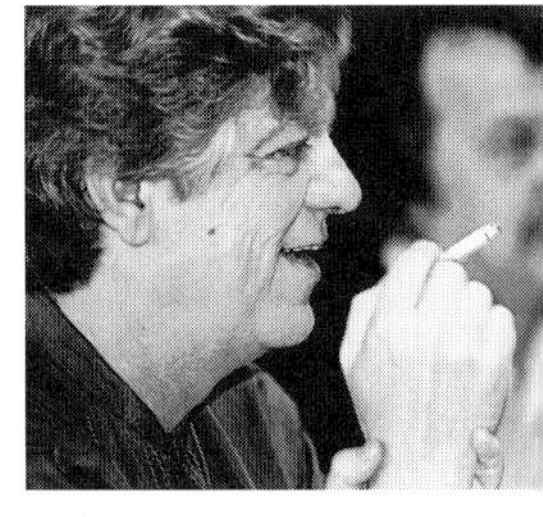
Lebbeus Woods

Zaha Hadid: It was very interesting what you said about hybrids. Recently there was a student competition for the Royal Institute of British Architects in London where the theme was hybrids. In seven hundred entries, there wasn't one interesting juxtaposition of two programs – even if they were bizarre. It was really extraordinary.
Eric Moss: It may actually happen in the worst scenarios. For instance, in the United States, when you see these institutions that don't work any more – the schools, the school boards, the libraries – and everything starts to deteriorate, finally somebody comes in desperately, and says, "Listen, we've got to remake these." Then you start to reinvent combinations, or recombine things, in a way make new programs. And that might engender an enormous amount of building, and new building, and new cities. But I think it will only happen when the alternative is catastrophe. Maybe then you might see an attempt to jump into something quite novel.

A Crisis of Meaning

Lebbeus Woods: Since you spoke of hybrid programs, what I've been trying to deal with is the emptiness, the cultural emptiness. When I say that I cannot accept a doctrine or ideology, or even the idea of the culture I live in, maybe it's only my problem. Nevertheless, it is real. How do you deal with that in terms of architecture? If you can believe in a hospital-and-discothèque hybrid, and maybe you can, at least you have a shred left of a belief in the whole structure that supports that. Sure, I do too, on a pragmatic level – if I hurt myself I am going to go to a hospital – but, on the other hand, in my soul, in my spirit, I cannot simply accept these almost-emptied labels any longer. So, what then, when things become empty?

In my own work I've been trying to make this a virtue: to see the virtue in a kind of emptiness of meaning. One cannot adopt or simply assume a meaning, one has to propose a meaning, out of one's own experience, for a given situation. When I talk about "freespace" it is very much about a space that is empty, completely empty of meaning.
Wolf Prix: Empty of meaning?
Zaha Hadid: Meaningless.
Wolf Prix: You are drawing meaningless space, or talking about it?
Zaha Hadid: But what does that mean?
Lebbeus Woods: Ha! That's good, Zaha! I love it, "What does that mean?"

Zaha Hadid

Eric Moss: I haven't seen any of those drawings of yours of meaningless space.
Lebbeus Woods: You haven't been looking.
Zaha Hadid: But what do you mean, meaningless space? It's a word game.
Lebbeus Woods: It is not a word game. I'll tell you something. If you design a space that no one has asked for, that no one demands or needs ...
Zaha Hadid: That is not meaningsless.
Lebbeus Woods: Why do you say so? If no one assigns any meaning, if the society assigns no meaning to it, where does the meaning come from?
Thom Mayne: It's embodied in the work ...
Wolf Prix: From you, Leb. Because you are drawing it.
Lebbeus Woods: The only reason I raise the subject, is the idea of new programs. So maybe one new program for architecture is emptiness.
Zaha Hadid: Do you mean emptiness in a void sense?
Lebbeus Woods: No, just emptiness.
Thom Mayne: This brings back the stuff that Tschumi was showing two days ago [in London]. There could be a discussion about neutrality ...
Lebbeus Woods: No, I am not talking about neutrality, neutrality is different.
Eric Moss: A lot of Tschumi's space, which had all kinds of assigned program, was the most meaningless and empty space ... It is true!
Wolf Prix: Empty, yeah, because people don't want to go there!
Lebbeus Woods: Nice joke. But I would like to define those terms better. I think Tschumi's work has to do with neutral space. In his lecture he, himself, talked about multifunctional space.
Eric Moss: Look, we started to talk about something, and we are getting very confused; you are talking about lack of meaning. You are making a space which is not defined programmatically. Yet, if you build it, it will come to be defined programmatically. If you dare to build it!
Lebbeus Woods: No, no.
Eric Moss: ...Because people are going to come to do things with it. They're going to climb on it, bite it, sleep in it ...
Lebbeus Woods: That's different, that's very different!
Eric Moss: So they'll do the programming for you! So don't worry about it!
Lebbeus Woods: Exactly! Eric, you understand perfectly!

A New Meaning for Program?

Lebbeus Woods: Regardless of whether it is hybrid, or "freespace," or some other idea of new program, I think this is something the architect needs to be very engaged in. In fact, I think that all of the architects who are here are already engaged in that process: in a sense writing a new program through the shaping of space. What I would hope for, what I am asking for, is not to cloak this in the language of lies, in the language of subterfuge ...

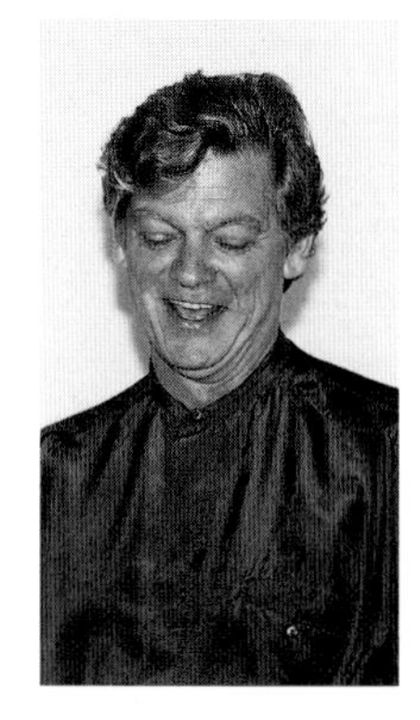
Lebbeus Woods

Eric Moss: I don't know what you're implying with "lying." Let me explain something: this guy makes a theater, and he sticks in a piece that, if you're reading the program, isn't asked for on the list. But this piece has a very substantial meaning in terms of how it is used, inhabited, and understood. It might have meanings the architect didn't foresee. And the client comes along and says, "Now wait a minute, it's not in the budget, it's not in the program," and so the architect says, "Well, we [could] have this carnival once a year, we'll bring in everybody, we'll make a lot of money for the city!" And therefore the guy says okay, and he builds it. And it's built ...

Lebbeus Woods: Okay, Fine.

Eric Moss: ... And that's the objective: *to get it built.* You can't sit there attacking the opposition and all of their weapons, and then decide you won't use any of their weapons. Unless you're Jesus Christ! What's the point? You never get anything done that way.

Zaha Hadid: Writing a program, and I've done this with students for ten years, was always the most exciting aspect of the work, the most demanding and, fundamentally, the most difficult. I agree that the focus should be on program, on how one rewrites program.

... When [Carme Pinós] was talking about interpreting the brief, and twisting it, that's one way to deal with the client. The trick with clients is to make them think you give them what they want, but actually you don't.

Carme Pinós

Steven Holl: I would just expand that idea of program one step, and actually cite a review I was on with Leb. His program was "laboratory of light." What's interesting is [the contrast with] this notion that program has only to do with function, just so many uses lined up ...

Zaha Hadid: Don't confuse program and function. They're very different.

Steven Holl: Exactly. When we're using the word program, we're using it in an open way, as something that needs to be re-invented.

A Note on Education

Steven Holl: Zaha was speaking about something that I want to reassert: the degree of self-indulgence imposed on the students by the teachers is creating a void. As an educator, I think experimentation is one thing, but when it becomes so divorced as to be just a total self-indulgence, there really is no dialogue possible.

Zaha Hadid: It's the triumph of the marginal, that's the problem. I think that there was a generation that did not believe in intelligence, and any form of culture ... [laughter]

Eric Moss: More than one generation!
Zaha Hadid: . . . It's a fact, and the [students today] are taught by people who, I am sorry to sound so strong about it, are crippled in a sense. The only way they can deal with educating these students is to tell them not to depict anything outside the walls of the school, because everything is bad; [they teach] without any critical sensibility, without being critical in a positive way.

All of the [students] are trying to resurrect their intuitive sensibility, but that is like the wet dream of a teenage girl – it's very weak. It's a major problem, the condition of education at this point.

Thom Mayne

In Closing

Frank Werner: We now have to come to an end, because the press is already waiting . . .
Zaha Hadid: You're getting pressed.
Lebbeus Woods: All right, pressed and not depressed.
Wolf Prix: Suppressed!
Frank Werner: We need to come to a final image, something like a thesis.
Thom Mayne: I don't think it's possible. I thought it would be useful if we could come up with some kind of agreed-upon agenda as to what the issues are; even whether it was possible to define an agenda – which would mean there's a collective enterprise, at least among the people at this table.
Steven Holl: There are a lot of elements of agreement here, right in front of us. This idea of a new architecture that allows for indeterminacy – I think everyone [here] is working on it. This is a radical thing, the idea of an architecture that embraces indeterminacy, whether it's in freespace, in the program, or in other ways. This is a continuity.
Wolf Prix: I would like to follow up on the term "hybrid program," and replace it with a better word, complexity. Then I have to ask, how can we reach this complexity? And I'm still at the argument I brought at the beginning that I think we can't reach complexity with multi-functional, "additive" thinking. You have to get rid of certain conventional terms in architecture, which arose from the nineteenth century. If you are stuck in the terms of a traditional way of thinking, only [a limited kind of] architecture will come out.

So, we have to imply more in our way of designing and thinking than was there before, otherwise we can't reach this complexity, freespace, open architecture, hybrid, or even the personal thinking. If you think in a very personal way, you use more than just rationality. Maybe you use your unconscious, as well as your conscious mind . . .

Steven Holl

Thom Mayne: That's one of the things I want to get back to: whether it's possible to produce an architecture that deals with indeterminacy and complexity, which includes figuration or type.

Wolf Prix: This is a discussion we had. You think it is possible ...

Thom Mayne: I think it is absolutely possible.

Eric Moss: What is the point? Is the point whether you can do it, or whether there is a way of explaining it?

Wolf Prix: Exploring it.

Eric Moss: A lot of the things you are talking about, one could work with and wouldn't necessarily need to label. It wouldn't matter what you called it.

Wolf Prix: My problem with architecture nowadays is that it's only architecture. When we go in for a program that is undetermined, or for undetermined space, or freespace, we have to apply a better vocabulary, which may facilitate a multi-layered way of thinking and seeing things. But we were trained in a very classical way. Our education is a very historical one. We learned one plus one is two, but there have been a lot of inventions, even in our century, like psychoanalysis or Cubism, which imply more than this "additive" thinking.

Thom Mayne: There's not a person at this table who thinks one plus one equals two who would come to that conclusion ...

Wolf Prix: Wait a minute ... verbally, that may be true. Even Leon Krier would agree. Rob Krier would claim he's "doing complexity ..."

Thom Mayne: I would say you're adding another subject to the agenda that has to do with the roles of strategy and methodology, and it's yet another discussion.

Wolf Prix: Thom, I would like to get rid of "typology"; I would like to get rid of this word "axis," and replace them with very strange words. We had the discussion about words we've never heard. A hammer and a nail is not necessary anymore, I say; I like the term "laboratory of light" – it leaves a lot of things open.

Thom Mayne: You can call an apple a zinker, but you've still got an apple.

Wolf Prix: No, just one minute. If we name this conference, we shouldn't follow the other examples. We should have another way. It's not a book, it's a magazine. It's not a book, it's just characters – something like that. I would propose that we find another way to communicate, so it's not a repetition of what we've already had.

Lebbeus Woods: The language we use is very important. You asked the question, Eric, is the point what we do, or how we describe what we do. Both are extremely important ...

Eric Moss: If the conference is a political act, and the intention is to deliver to the outside a statement which alters the perception of architecture in our favor, then Wolf is saying, "Find a way to present the content that allows us to move the discussion in our direction, in our favor, in a way somebody else can understand."

Wolf Prix: Right, right, I agree.

Eric Moss

Lebbeus Woods: But this is where I think you and Wolf differ. Wolf is saying we have to invent new words and convince people of their validity. We can't talk about cave paintings and Ptolemy to try to convince people, because as soon as we invoke those archetypes, we place our own ideas back in the realm of that archaic world. The world we are talking about is not that archaic world.

Eric Moss: There is one other possibility, which is not to say what we would say ...

Lebbeus Woods: But to lie ... [laughter]

Eric Moss: ... but to say what you *wouldn't* say, what is *not* tolerable among the various ways of formulating architecture conceptually. So, if you're tired of layering, it's a term you reject. Then in the process of making work intelligible, the "offending" terms are eliminated. Otherwise, what Wolf is advocating is another vocabulary that in twenty minutes will be as bad as the last one.

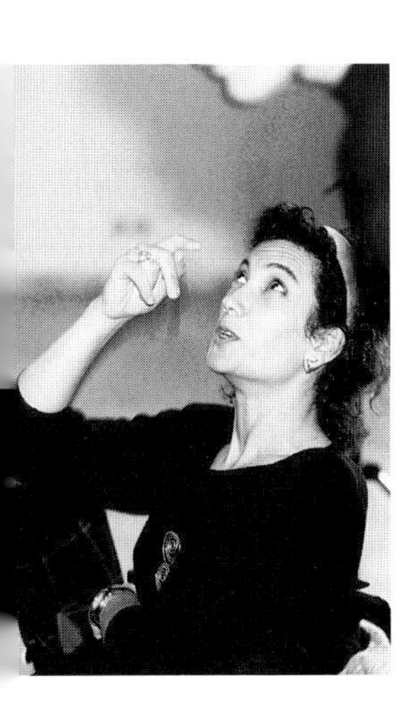

Carme Pinós

Lebbeus Woods: It will get us through the next time frame, that's all. There's nothing that's going to be eternal. We're not looking for eternal verities.

Wolf Prix: I've got a good example of what I mean. One of the students is doing a thesis about virtual reality, and another student said, "Why don't you call this project 'Could Virtual Space Burn?'" It has nothing to do with architecture anymore. It puts a question and an answer in the same sentence; [this is something we] were talking about the other night: a transitional language, which is a hybrid as well. The transitional words are getting more and more important. This could be a tool, like a transitional designing process. It could be a tool to create these things we are going for.

Carme Pinós: One of the things I want to say is that maybe our mistake is that we want too much to be protagonists, to make an architecture of protagonism. Architecture should communicate with the people who use it.

I recently traveled to America, and visited [Kahn's] library at Exeter. It's fantastic. It's like a movie. The movement of people inside – this is the architecture, not the volume.

And maybe our mistake is to ask the architecture to explain all. In the cemetery project I showed, it is the way people walk through it and react to it that is the architecture.

Helmut Swiczinsky: The cemetery couldn't have happened if there had been an opinion poll.

Steven Holl: This is something we brought up earlier. This could also be a point that comes from this conference: architecture cannot be subject to a democratic vote.

Helmut Swiczinsky

Helmut Swiczinsky: I'd like to hear that people understood your notions about what architecture could express, that they found it in the architecture. We trust that architecture can do that, but we are very suspicious that it can be decided on an "additive" opinion poll method. All of us are

trying this complex, open-architecture idea. Therefore we have the same problem, because political programmatics still work on an additive, counting basis. No politician can wait for four years, until the architecture is proved by people's experience of the work.
Carme Pinós: Maybe we must educate not only the client, but also other architects. In Barcelona ten years ago all the bars and restaurants were awful – they were all like the Hilton. A few designers started to make things differently. All the architects now try to make things differently. I am an optimist ...
Helmut Swiczinsky: It's about building. Zaha said she'd done all the double-page publishing to learn how to build the fire station. If it works, it's worthwhile.
Zaha Hadid: Architecture is a very slow thing.
Helmut Swiczinsky: Very heavy ...
Wolf Prix: We should say *arquitectura es muerta, viva la arquitectura* ...
Lebbeus Woods: Let me raise one final question, which Zaha actually provoked with her comment. If it takes time to develop this new program, this new client, or as Thom mentioned, some kind of new position – I mean, if we have something in common, it's going to take a while to find out what it is and also to articulate the differences.

Then what about the next time we meet? When will that happen, and where? Or, should it happen? Is this it? This was the event and that's the end of history?
Peter Noever: Or is it the end of traveling? [laughter]
Lebbeus Woods: No, but I'm serious. For myself I would say that this has been in a curious way very enlightening and productive. We've all met each other before, talked about airplane tickets and all sorts of odd things in funny places, but this is the first time in my experience that we've sat down and actually taken up issues.

There have been some strong disagreements, which I'm glad for. But on the other hand I think we do have something in common. I think there is something that could be said eventually.

Some of you talked about a relationship to the human race, to people, and I agree with you, I feel that also. Maybe we haven't come terribly close to defining that today, maybe we never will. But I somehow feel that these very honest and direct discussions are useful. Do we want to do this again, or not?
Zaha Hadid: If we meet again, we have to make sure that the words we use mean the same to all of us ...
Lebbeus Woods: That's a process.
Zaha Hadid: When people talk about program, they have to state what program is. When we say politics, we should say what we mean by it.
Eric Moss: In a very simple way, if we're looking for a definition, my definition of what this sort of convocation is about is protecting certain people, and making it possible for them to continue to do a certain kind of work.

Peter Noever

1
In 1988, fourteen American architects competed for the design of a German-funded addition to the American Memorial Library in Berlin. Steven Holl, Karen Van Lengen, and Lars Lerup were chosen as first-place winners in the first phase. The three developed their schemes further and in April 1989 Holl's design was selected. In early 1990, political changes in Berlin – including the defeat of the Social Democratic city government that had steered the original competition – led to the rejection of the Holl scheme by Wolfgang Nagel, the new senator in charge of building, and the premiation of Van Lengen's design.

Steven Holl: I disagree. I think there's a much more open possibility here, which has to do with a different kind of order, different kinds of programs, and a different kind of client. We're in the middle of a cultural situation which is in dynamic change. The whole world is in one of the most dynamic moments, and I think as architects we need to re-form our positions, which in some way are a parallel. Then those new clients could emerge; when we speak about an architecture that is against hegemony, against a kind of symmetrical ordering, we can make a parallel in politics. There could be some kind of connection that could be made. It takes a little work ...

Lebbeus Woods: If this group of so-called individualists could at least agree on a next step, or a next meeting even, I think it would have a tremendous effect in terms of creating this dialogue with a wider public. We are not close to it yet, but it is possible.

Steven Holl: Being in Vienna, I also feel a little bit closer to the center of this dynamic change in the globe; when I am sitting in Los Angeles or in New York, I feel that we are stuck with the problems of America. I think the problems are global, too; and there is an architecture that's about to be formed to somehow give some shape to this. Maybe next time we should meet in Istanbul, where the Orient and Occident meet, right at the cusp!

Zaha Hadid: Maybe we should all meet separately and talk about these things. I haven't seen many of you for a long time, and nothing like this has been done for a long time ...

But I go back to my observations about certain tendencies in London. There are meetings which [amount to] a negation of architecture but, on the other hand, there are political meetings which are almost underground ... They are "submerged" in seminars on economics, conferences on literature and writing, Marxist writing; there could be another kind of audience that one could begin to engage, which is a mixed audience, not this architectural audience ...

It seems to me that this would be the other way to intertwine the architectural scene with other people, without making confusion. It is important to confront issues of architecture with issues of culture, and politics, and people. One has to add, in time, other things to it. I think we should meet again. You can come to my house ...

2

Sponsored by the City of Vienna, a competition for the revitalization of the landmarked Ronacher Theater was held in 1986 with the participation of fifteen Austrian architects. In 1987, Coop Himmelblau won the competition with a scheme that entailed the remodeling of the existing auditorium to enhance its staging capabilities, and the addition of a new, functionally flexible space at the top of the structure. In Autumn 1991, the City of Vienna cancelled the project, stating that it was too costly to build.

3

B. Braun Melsungen Industrial Plant, in Melsungen bei Kassel, Germany, by Walter Nageli in association with Stirling, Wilford & Associates.

4

In 1989 the Settore Architettura of the Venice Biennale invited a dozen architects to design a new facility on the Lido to house the Venice Film Festival. Steven Holl proposed a vast artificial grotto, defined by a U-shaped plan open to the canal, with six large cinemas spanning the gap overhead. The irregular forms of the "levitating" cinemas created fissures that allowed light to pierce the grotto, which was conceived as a watery entrance court.

Biographies

COOP HIMMELBLAU

Coop Himmelblau was founded in 1968 in Vienna by Wolf D. Prix (born in Vienna in 1942) and Helmut Swiczinsky (born in Poznan, Poland, in 1944). In 1991, Frank Stepper (born in Stuttgart in 1955) became a member of the group.

In 1989, Prix and Swiczinsky opened a second office in Los Angeles. The same year saw construction begin on the "Open House" in California; in 1991, work began on the "Rehak House" in Malibu.

Completed projects include the "Funder Factory" in St. Veit/Glan, Kärnten (Austria), and the attic conversion in Falkestrasse, Vienna, as well as the Europaplatz Center in St. Pölten (competition, 1991). In 1987, Coop Himmelblau won two major competitions: the international urban design competition for Melun-Sénart, a suburb south of Paris; and the competition for the conversion of the Ronacher Theater in Vienna (this latter project, however, was abandoned by the city of Vienna for financial reasons in 1991). In 1992, the architects took first prize for the "Obere Tor" (Main Gate) in Bietigheim-Bissingen, and for the "German Hygiene Museum" in Dresden.

Coop Himmelblau's work has been shown in many international exhibitions, including the show "Deconstructivist Architecture" at the Museum of Modern Art, in New York (1988), and "Construire le Ciel" (To Build the Heavens) at the Centre Georges Pompidou, Paris (1992/93). They have lectured or taught as visiting professors at universities in Europe (where they led the architecture class at the School of Applied Arts in Vienna), Japan, Australia, and the United States. The architects live and work in Vienna and Los Angeles.

ZAHA HADID

Born in 1950 in Baghdad, Iraq, Zaha Hadid studied mathematics at the American University in Beirut, and architecture at the Architectural Association School of Architecture in London (1972–77) under Leon Krier, Jeremy Dixon, and Rem Koolhaas. From 1976 to 1978 she was a member of the group OMA (Office for Metropolitan Architecture), and subsequently opened her own office in London. She has taught at the Architectural Association (1977–86), at Harvard University, Cambridge (1986), and at Columbia University in New York (1987).

Zaha Hadid won first prize in the international competition for "The Peak" in Hong Kong (1983) as well as for the "Trafalgar Square Grand Buildings Project" (1985). Recent projects include the "Vitra Fire Station" in Weil am Rhein, Germany (1993), and the "Rhein Harbor Art and Media Center" in Düsseldorf, Germany (1992). She is known for her expressive design sketches and free-space studies.

Her work has appeared in numerous group and one-woman shows, including "Deconstructivist Architecture" at the Museum of Modern Art,

New York (1988), and a group show at the Max Protetch Gallery, New York (1989).

Hadid lives and works in London.

STEVEN HOLL

Born in Seattle in 1948, Steven Holl studied in Rome, in London, and at the University of Washington, and founded his New York architectural office in 1978. As the head architect, he is responsible for the office's designs for architecture and urban planning.

Even early projects, such as the "Museum of Modern Art Tower" in New York (1986), are distinguished by a formal/minimalist tendency and stand for architectural clarity and simplicity.

Later works, including the "D. E. Shaw & Co. Offices" in New York (1991), are characterized by constructivist elements, by a reduction of light and color, and by the way they integrate their natural surroundings, as exemplified by the design for the "Texas Stretto House" in Dallas, Texas (1992). He has had exhibitions and produced publications in the U.S., Europe, and the Far East. Among other numerous honorable distinctions, he received the American Institute of Architects Chapter Award in 1985.

In 1989, Holl became a professor at the Columbia University Graduate School of Architecture and Planning in New York, where he now lives and works.

THOM MAYNE

Born in 1944, Thom Mayne studied at the University of Southern California and at the Harvard Graduate School of Design. In 1974, together with Michael Rotondi, he founded the architectural office Morphosis, intended to represent new links between man and nature, and to investigate the definition of architecture as a social art. In 1992 he left Morphosis and founded his own architectural firm in Los Angeles.

The residential "Sixth Street House" in Los Angeles (1986) is an intensive dialogue with its pre-existing surroundings. The "Crawford Residence" in Montecito, Los Angeles (1987), is an exemplary illustration of perfect harmony between a spectacular setting and a sheltered family home. With the "Comprehensive Cancer Clinic" in Los Angeles (1987), the architects intended to create an environment far different from the usual hospital atmosphere.

Recent competitions include the "Yuzen Vintage Car Museum" in Los Angeles (1992), and the "Cranbrook Gatehouse Competition" (1992). Thom Mayne has taught at Yale University (1991) and Harvard University (1992).

Other realized projects include the "72 Market Street Restaurant" in

Venice, California (1983), and the "Kate Mantilini Restaurant" in Los Angeles (1986).

Mayne lives and works in Santa Monica, California.

ERIC OWEN MOSS

Born in 1943, Eric Owen Moss studied architecture at the University of California at Berkeley and at Harvard University. Since 1974, he has been Professor of Design at the Southern California University of Architecture, where he is also on the Board of Directors. In 1976, he opened his own office in Culver City, California. He has received numerous awards, most recently the LA/AIA Design Award in 1990 for his Paramount Laundry Building (1987–89).

Next to Frank O. Gehry and Morphosis, Eric Owen Moss is one of the most important representatives of new California architecture. One recurring theme in his work is the dialogue with pre-existing structures, evident in the conversion of an abandoned factory plant in Culver City (1986–90), or the former industrial building Lindblade Tower in Culver City (1987–89). The use of elements of industrial mass production and dissonances point to the development of a new aesthetic.

Recent projects include the "P & D Guest House" in Los Angeles (1992), the "Samitaur Offices" in Los Angeles (1993), "Rhino Records Headquarters" in Culver City (1993), and the "Westen Lawson House" in Los Angeles.

Moss lives and works in Culver City, California.

CARME PINÓS

Born in 1954, Carme Pinós co-founded an architectural office with Enric Miralles (born in 1955) in 1984. Until their separation in 1991, they developed their individual, formal, and starkly functional designs.

Their first project, which received the FAD prize in 1987, was the conversion of the factory building La Llauna in Barcelona (1984–86). Other projects include the "Centro Social de Hostalets" in Barcelona (1986–92), "Vall d'Hebron" in the Olympic sports arena, Barcelona (1991), "Igualada Cemetery" near Barcelona (1991), "Sports Hall and Grounds" in Huesca, Catalonia (1988), and "Pedestrian Bridge" in Lérida (1985).

Pinós is based in Barcelona.

LEBBEUS WOODS

Lebbeus Woods was born in 1940 in Lansing, Michigan, and studied at the Purdue University School of Engineering and the University of Illinois School of Architecture. His intense preoccupation with architectural theory and experimental architecture is evidenced by a wide range of publications which have appeared since 1976, including *Architecture, Sculpture, Painting Series* (1979), *Einstein Tomb* (1980), and *AEON: The Architecture of Time* (1982), as well as by lectures in the United States and Europe at such venues as Harvard and Columbia Universities, the Architectural Association in London, and, currently, at Cooper Union in New York.

Recent projects include the "Zagreb Free Zone" (1991; see statement below), "Zagreb Free Space Structure" (1991), "Berlin Free Zone" (1990), "Aerial Paris" (1989), and "Solo House" (1989), all of which demonstrate Woods's interest in questions of free space and kinetic architecture.

Lebbeus Woods has been featured in a number of one-man and group shows, including "At the Edge of Chaos: New Images of the World" at the Louisiana Museum of Modern Art, Copenhagen (1993); "Terra Nova: Drawings and Models of Lebbeus Woods" at the MIT List Visual Arts Center, Cambridge (1992); "Architecture is a Political Act" at the Gund Hall Gallery, Harvard University (1991); "Zagreb Free Zone" at the Museum of Arts and Crafts, Zagreb, Croatia (1991); "Berlin Free Zone" at the Aedes Galerie, Berlin (1991); and "Artists' Houses" at the Architecture Museum in Frankfurt (1989).

In 1988, together with Olive Brown, Lebbeus Woods founded the non-profit Research Institute for Experimental Architecture, dedicated to the practice-oriented exploration and support of experimental architecture. He has lived and worked in New York since 1976.

Zagreb Free Zone Project – Statement by the Architect

The Zagreb Free Zone project was conceived as an architecture of liberation, introducted into a Yugoslavia and Croatia in transition from Communism to a new – as of the 1991 exhibition in which this project was introduced – undefined condition of autonomy. The experimental and provocative concepts of *heterarchy*, *free zone* and *freespace*, devoloped first in projects for Paris and Berlin, were offered at a critical historical moment in Yugoslavia, with the intention that they would initiate a dialogue and a constructive means of social and political transformation that the making of architecture uniquely provides. The ensuing war destroyed any hope for the realization of those intentions. Nationalism and authoritarian government in Croatia, leading to profoundly questionable machinations with regard to the war-tortured, newly independent nation of Bosnia-Herzegovina, as well as the suppression of free speech in Croatia, have obviated the underlying concepts of the Zagreb Free Zone project.

My efforts as an architect have turned to the critical human issues raised by the destruction of human community caused by violence and war. The War and Architecture Series, begun at the time Sarajevo came under siege, examines the dual role of architecture with regard to war: first, as a contributor to war, insofar as it is normally aligned with institutions of authority, wealth, and power, the very instigators of war; secondly, as an instrument of the reconstruction of war-devastated cities. In the former regard, this series of drawings and models reveals the ethical and phenomenological ambiguity inherent in the concept of construction. In the latter regard, it posits a reconstructive architecture based not on replacement of what has been lost, but on the making of new patterns of thought and living arising from an architecture constructed on the existential remnants of war. The hope persists of re-estab-lishing – on the ancient human landscape – a complex society, founded on dialogue, tolerance, and diversity.

Photographic Acknowledgments

Photographs not included in this list were taken from the architects' archives.

Hélène Binet p. 24, 33 (bottom)
Tom Bonner p. 23, 52–53, 56, 66 (bottom), 68–69, 71 (top)
Steven Chen p. 54–55
Todd Conversano p. 60, 66 (bottom), 68–70, 71 (top)
Peter Cook p. 68 (bottom), 69
Tim Street-Porter p. 68 (bottom), 69
Hisao Suzuki p. 72, 74–75
Alex Vertikoff p. 60, 68 (bottom), 69
Paul Warchol p. 34, 38–41
Gertrud Wolfschwenger p. 21
Gerald Zugmann p. 16, 22